SMITH WIGGLESWORTH

Only **Believe**

Other Titles by Smith Wigglesworth

SMITH WIGGLESWORTH

Only **Believe**

Experience God's Miracles Every Day

WHITAKER
HOUSE

Whitaker House gratefully acknowledges and thanks Glenn Gohr and the entire staff of the Assemblies of God Archives in Springfield, Missouri, for graciously assisting us in compiling Smith Wigglesworth's works for publication in this book.

Publisher's note: This new edition from Whitaker House has been updated for the modern reader. Words, expressions, and sentence structure have been revised for clarity and readability. Although the more modern Bible translation quoted in this edition was not available to the author, the Bible versions used were prayerfully selected in order to make the language of the entire text readily understandable while maintaining the author's original premises and message.

Unless otherwise indicated, all Scripture quotations are taken from the *New King James Version*, © 1979, 1980, 1982, 1984 by Thomas Nelson, Inc. Used by permission. All rights reserved. Scripture quotations marked (KJV) are taken from the King James Version of the Holy Bible.

Smith Wigglesworth ONLY BELIEVE:
Experience God's Miracles Every Day
(Previously published as *Smith Wigglesworth on Power to Serve*)

ISBN-13: 978-0-88368-996-7
ISBN-10: 0-88368-996-0
Printed in the United States of America
© 1998 by Whitaker House

1030 Hunt Valley Circle
New Kensington, PA 15068
www.whitakerhouse.com

Library of Congress Cataloging-in-Publication Data
Wigglesworth, Smith, 1859–1947.
Smith Wigglesworth only believe : experience God's miracles every day / by Smith Wigglesworth.—New ed.
p. cm.
Rev. ed. of: Smith Wigglesworth on power to serve. ©1998.
Summary: "An exploration of the power of active belief and how to develop simple, childlike faith in God and His Word"—Provided by publisher.
ISBN-13: 978-0-88368-996-7 (trade pbk. : alk. paper)
ISBN-10: 0-88368-996-0 (trade pbk. : alk. paper)
1. Spiritual life. I. Wigglesworth, Smith, 1859–1947. Smith Wigglesworth on power to serve. II. Title.
BV4501.3.W5423 2006
252'.0994—dc22   2005031079

3 4 5 6 7 8 9 10 11 **uı** 14 13 12 11 10 09 08 07

Contents

Introduction

An encounter with Smith Wigglesworth was an unforgettable experience. This seems to be the universal reaction of all who knew him or heard him speak. Smith Wigglesworth was a simple yet remarkable man who was used in an extraordinary way by our extraordinary God. He had a contagious and inspiring faith. Under his ministry, thousands of people came to salvation, committed themselves to a deeper faith in Christ, received the baptism in the Holy Spirit, and were miraculously healed. The power that brought these kinds of results was the presence of the Holy Spirit, who filled Smith Wigglesworth and used him in bringing the good news of the Gospel to people all over the world. Wigglesworth gave glory to God for everything that was accomplished through his ministry, and he wanted people to understand his work only in this context, because his sole desire was that people would see Jesus and not himself.

Smith Wigglesworth was born in England in 1859. Immediately after his conversion as a boy, he had a concern for the salvation of others and won people to Christ, including his mother. Even so, as a young man, he could not express himself well enough to give a testimony in church, much less preach a sermon. Wigglesworth said that his mother had the same difficulty in expressing herself that he did. This family trait, coupled with the fact that he had no formal education because he began working twelve hours a day at the age of seven to help support the family, contributed to Wigglesworth's awkward speaking style. He became a plumber by trade, yet he continued to devote himself to winning many people to Christ on an individual basis.

In 1882, he married Polly Featherstone, a vivacious young woman who loved God and had a gift of preaching and evangelism. It was she who taught him to read and who became his closest confidant and strongest supporter. They both had compassion for the poor and needy in their community, and they opened a mission, at which Polly preached. Significantly, people were miraculously healed when Wigglesworth prayed for them.

In 1907, Wigglesworth's circumstances changed dramatically when, at the age of forty-eight, he was baptized in the Holy Spirit. Suddenly, he had a new power that enabled him to preach, and even his wife was amazed at the transformation. This was the beginning of what became a worldwide evangelistic and healing ministry that reached thousands. He eventually ministered in the United States, Australia, South Africa, and all over Europe. His ministry extended up to the time of his death in 1947.

Several emphases in Smith Wigglesworth's life and ministry characterize him: a genuine, deep compassion for the unsaved and sick; an unflinching belief in the Word of God; a desire that Christ should increase and he should decrease (see John 3:30); a belief that he was called to exhort people to enlarge their faith and trust in God; an emphasis on the baptism in the Holy Spirit with the manifestation of the gifts of the Spirit as in the early church; and a belief in complete healing for everyone of all sickness.

Smith Wigglesworth was called "The Apostle of Faith" because absolute trust in God was a constant theme of both his life and his messages. In his meetings, he would quote passages from the Word of God and lead lively singing to help build people's faith and encourage them to act on it. He emphasized belief in the fact that God could do the impossible. He had great faith in what God could do, and God did great things through him.

Wigglesworth's unorthodox methods were often questioned. As a person, Wigglesworth was reportedly courteous, kind, and gentle. However, he became forceful when dealing with the Devil, whom he believed caused all sickness. Wigglesworth said the reason he spoke bluntly and acted forcefully with people was that he knew he needed to get their attention so they could focus on God.

He also had such anger toward the Devil and sickness that he acted in a seemingly rough way. When he prayed for people to be healed, he would often hit or punch them at the place of their problem or illness. Yet, no one was hurt by this startling treatment. Instead, they were remarkably healed. When he was asked why he treated people in this manner, he said that he was not hitting the people but that he was hitting the Devil. He believed that Satan should never be treated gently or allowed to get away with anything. About twenty people were reportedly raised from the dead after he prayed for them. Wigglesworth himself was healed of appendicitis and kidney stones, after which his personality softened and he was gentler with those who came to him for prayer for healing. His abrupt manner in ministering may be attributed to the fact that he was very serious about his calling and got down to business quickly.

Although Wigglesworth believed in complete healing, he encountered illnesses and deaths that were difficult to understand. These included the deaths of his wife and son, his daughter's lifelong deafness, and his own battles with kidney stones and sciatica.

He often seemed paradoxical: compassionate but forceful, blunt but gentle, a well-dressed gentleman whose speech was often ungrammatical or confusing. However, he loved God with everything he had, he was steadfastly committed to God and to His Word, and he didn't rest until he saw God move in the lives of those who needed Him.

In 1936, Smith Wigglesworth prophesied about what we now know as the charismatic movement. He accurately predicted that the established mainline denominations would experience revival and the gifts of the Spirit in a way that would surpass even the Pentecostal movement. Wigglesworth did not live to see the renewal, but as an evangelist and prophet with a remarkable healing ministry, he had a tremendous influence on both the Pentecostal and charismatic movements, and his example and influence on believers is felt to this day.

Without the power of God that was so obviously present in his life and ministry, we might not be reading transcripts of his sermons, for his spoken messages were often disjointed and ungrammatical. However, true gems of spiritual insight shine through them because of the revelation he received through the Holy Spirit. It was his life of complete devotion and belief in God and his reliance on the Holy Spirit that brought the life-changing power of God into his messages.

As you read this book, it is important to remember that Wigglesworth's works span a period of several decades, from the early 1900s to the 1940s. They were originally presented as spoken rather than written messages, and necessarily retain some of the flavor of a church service or prayer meeting. Some of the messages were Bible studies that Wigglesworth led at various conferences. At his meetings, he would often speak in tongues and give the interpretation, and these messages have been included as well. Because of Wigglesworth's unique style, the sermons and Bible studies in this book have been edited for clarity, and archaic expressions that would be unfamiliar to modern readers have been updated.

In conclusion, we hope that as you read these words of Smith Wigglesworth, you will truly sense his complete trust and unwavering faith in God and take to heart one of his favorite sayings: "Only believe!"

one

The Dispensation of the Holy Spirit

hese are the days of the dispensation of the Holy Spirit. I find in the book of Galatians that there is a very blessed way to receive the Holy Spirit:

> *That the blessing of Abraham might come upon the Gentiles in Christ Jesus, that we might receive the promise of the Spirit through faith.* (Galatians 3:14)

When we have the right attitude, faith becomes remarkably active. But it can never be remarkably active in a dead life. When sin is out, when the body is clean, and when the life is made right, then the Holy Spirit comes, and faith brings the evidence.

Why should we tarry, or wait, for the Holy Spirit? Why should we wrestle and pray with a living faith to be made ready? In the book of John, we find the reason:

13

*Nevertheless I tell you the truth. It is to
your advantage that I go away; for if I do
not go away, the Helper will not come to
you; but if I depart, I will send Him to you.
And when He has come, He will convict
the world of sin, and of righteousness, and
of judgment.* (John 16:7–8)

To convict the world of sin, righteousness,
and judgment—that is why the Holy Spirit is to
come into your body. First
of all, your sin is gone,
and you can see clearly to
speak to others. But Jesus
does not want you to point
out the speck in somebody
else's eye while the plank
is in your own. (See Matthew 7:3–5.) When your
own sins are gone, then
the Holy Spirit is to convince the world of sin, of righteousness, and of
judgment.

> The place of
> being filled
> with the Holy
> Spirit is where
> the believer
> binds the power
> of Satan.

The place of being filled with the Holy Spirit
is the only place of operation where the believer
binds the power of Satan. Satan thinks that he
has a right, and he will have a short time to exhibit that right as the Prince of the World; but
he can't be Prince as long as there is one person
filled with the Holy Spirit. That is the reason that
the church will go before the Tribulation.

Now, how dare you resist coming into the place of being filled with the life and power of the Holy Spirit? I call you to halt, and then to march.

Halt! Think! What is the attitude of your life? Are you thirsty? Are you longing? Are you willing to pay the price? Are you willing to forfeit in order to have? Are you willing to allow yourself to die so that He may live? Are you willing for Him to have the right-of-way in your heart, your conscience, and all you are? Are you ready to have God's deluge of blessing upon your soul?

Are you ready? "What for?" you ask. To be changed forever, to receive the Holy Spirit, to be filled with divine power forever.

RECEIVING THE HOLY SPIRIT

If you would believe half as much as you ask, you would receive. Many people do not receive the Holy Spirit because they are continually asking and never believing.

> *Ask, and it will be given to you; seek, and you will find; knock, and it will be opened to you. For everyone who asks receives, and he who seeks finds, and to him who knocks it will be opened.* (Matthew 7:7–8)

"Everyone who asks receives." He who is asking is receiving; he who is seeking is finding. The door is being opened right now; that is God's present Word. The Bible does not say, "Ask and you will not receive." Believe that asking is receiving, seeking is finding, and to him who is knocking, the door is being opened.

Faith has its request. Faith claims it because it has it. *"Faith is the substance of things hoped for"* (Hebrews 11:1). As sure as you have faith, God will give you the overflowing, and when He comes in, you will speak as the Spirit gives utterance. (See Acts 2:4.)

two

Full of the Holy Spirit

esus says, *"Do not be afraid; only believe"* (Mark 5:36). The people in whom God delights are the ones who rest upon His Word without wavering. God has nothing for the man who doubts, for *"let not that man suppose that he will receive anything from the Lord"* (James 1:7). Therefore, I would like us to get this verse deep down into our hearts, until it penetrates every fiber of our being: *"Only believe!"* We know that *"all things are possible"* (Matthew 19:26). *"Only believe."*

God has a plan for this meeting, beyond anything that we have ever known before. He has a plan for every individual life, and if we have any other plan in view, we miss the grandest plan of all! Nothing in the past is equal to the present, and nothing in the present can equal the things of tomorrow, for tomorrow should be so filled with holy expectations that we will be living flames for God. God never intended His people to be ordinary or commonplace. His intentions were that they should be on fire for Him, conscious of His divine power, realizing the glory of the cross that foreshadows the crown.

THE STORY OF STEPHEN

God has given me a very special Scripture to share:

> *Now in those days, when the number of the disciples was multiplying, there arose a complaint against the Hebrews by the Hellenists, because their widows were neglected in the daily distribution. Then the twelve summoned the multitude of the disciples and said, "It is not desirable that we should leave the word of God and serve tables. Therefore, brethren, seek out from among you seven men of good reputation, full of the Holy Spirit and wisdom, whom we may appoint over this business...." And the saying pleased the whole multitude. And they chose Stephen, a man full of faith and the Holy Spirit, and Philip, Prochorus, Nicanor, Timon, Parmenas, and Nicolas, a proselyte from Antioch.*
>
> (Acts 6:1–3, 5)

During the time of the early church, the disciples were hard-pressed in all areas. The things of the natural life could not be attended to, and many were complaining about the neglect of their widows. The disciples therefore decided on a plan, which was to choose seven men to do the work—men who were "full of the Holy Spirit." What a divine thought! No matter what kind of work was to be done, however menial it may have been, the person chosen had to be filled with the Holy Spirit. The plan of the church was that everything, even the things of the natural life, had to be sanctified unto God, for the church had to be a Holy Spirit church.

Beloved, God has never ordained anything less! There is one thing that I want to stress in these meetings; that is, no matter what else may happen, first and foremost, I want to emphasize these questions: *"Have you received the Holy Spirit since you believed?"* (Acts 19:2 KJV). "Are you filled with divine power?" This is the heritage of the church, to be so clothed with power that God can lay His hand on any member at any time to do His perfect will.

There is no stopping in the Spirit-filled life. We begin at the cross—the place of ignominy, shame, and death—and that very death brings the power of resurrection life. And, being filled with the Holy Spirit, we go on *"from glory to glory"* (2 Corinthians 3:18). Let us not forget that possessing the baptism in the Holy Spirit means that there must be an ever increasing holiness in us.

How the church needs divine anointing—God's presence and power so manifested that the world will know it! People know when the tide is flowing; they also know when it is ebbing.

The necessity that seven men be chosen for the position of serving tables was very evident. The disciples knew that these seven men were men ready for active service, and so they chose them. In Acts 6:5, we read, *"And the saying pleased the whole multitude. And they chose Stephen, a man full of faith and the Holy Spirit, and Philip."* There were five others listed, of course, but Stephen and Philip stand out most prominently in the Scriptures. Philip was a man so filled with the Holy Spirit that a revival always followed wherever he went. Stephen was a man so filled with divine power that, although serving tables might have been all right in the minds of the other disciples, God had a greater vision for him—a baptism of fire, of power and divine anointing, that took him on and on to the climax of his life, until he saw right into the open heavens.

Had we been there with the disciples at that time, I believe we would have heard them saying to each other, "Look here! Neither Stephen nor Philip are doing the work we called them to. If they do not attend to business, we will have to get someone else!" That was the natural way of thinking, but divine order is far above our finite planning. When we please God in our daily activities, we will always find in operation the fact that *"he who is faithful in what is least* [God will make] *faithful also in much"* (Luke 16:10). We have such an example right here—a man chosen to serve tables who had such a revelation of the mind of Christ and of the depth and height of God that there was no pause in his experience, but a going forward with leaps and bounds. Beloved, there is a race to be run; there is a crown to be won; we cannot stand still! I say unto you, *"Be vigilant"* (1 Peter 5:8). Be vigilant! Let no one take your crown! (See Revelation 3:11.)

> God has privileged us in Christ Jesus to live above the ordinary human plane of life.

God has privileged us in Christ Jesus to live above the ordinary human plane of life. Those who want to be ordinary and live on a lower plane can do so, but as for me, I will not! For the same anointing, the same zeal, the same Holy Spirit power that was at the command of Stephen and the apostles is at our command. We have the same God that Abraham had, that Elijah had, and we do not need to come short in any gift or grace. (See 1 Corinthians 1:7.) We may not possess the gifts as abiding gifts, but as we are full of the Holy Spirit and divine anointing, it is possible, when there is need, for God to manifest every gift of the Spirit through us. As I have already said, I do not mean by this that we should necessarily possess the gifts permanently, but there should be a manifestation of the gifts as God may choose to use us.

This ordinary man Stephen became mighty under the Holy Spirit's anointing, and now he stands supreme, in many ways, among the apostles. *"And Stephen, full of faith and power, did great wonders and signs among the people"* (Acts 6:8). As we go deeper in God, He enlarges our understanding and places before us a wide-open door, and I am not surprised that this man chosen to serve tables was afterward called to a higher plane. "What do you mean?" you may ask. "Did he quit this service?" No! But he was lost in the power of God. He lost sight of everything in the natural and steadfastly fixed his gaze upon Jesus, *"the author and finisher of our faith"* (Hebrews 12:2), until he was transformed into a shining light in the kingdom of God.

Oh, that we might be awakened to believe His Word, to understand the mind of the Spirit, for there is an inner place of whiteness and purity where we can see God. Stephen was just as ordinary a person as you and I, but he was in the place where God could so move upon him that he, in turn, could move everything before him. He began in a most humble place and ended in a blaze of glory. Beloved, dare to believe Christ!

RESISTANCE TO THE HOLY SPIRIT

As you go on in this life of the Spirit, you will find that the Devil will begin to get restless and there will be a "stir in the synagogue," so to speak. It was so with Stephen. Any number of people may be found in the church who are very proper in a worldly sense—always properly dressed, the elite of the land, welcoming into the church everything but the power of God. Let us read what God says about them:

> *Then there arose some from what is called the Synagogue of the Freedmen (Cyrenians, Alexandrians, and those from Cilicia and Asia), disputing with Stephen. And they were not able to resist the wisdom and the Spirit by which he spoke.*
>
> (Acts 6:9–10)

The Freedmen could not stand the truth of God. With these opponents, Stephen found himself in the same predicament as the blind man whom Jesus had healed. (See John 9:1–34.) As soon as the blind man's eyes were opened, the religious leaders shut him out of the synagogue. They would not have anybody in the synagogue with his eyes open. It is the same today; as soon as you receive spiritual eyesight, out you go!

These Freedmen, Cyrenians, and Alexandrians rose up full of wrath in the very place where they should have been full of the power of God, full of divine love, and full of reverence for the Holy Spirit. They rose up against Stephen, this man who was *"full of the Holy Spirit"* (Acts 6:3).

Beloved, if there is anything in your life that in any way resists the power of the Holy Spirit and the entrance of His Word into your heart and life, drop on your knees and cry out loud for mercy! When the Spirit of God is brooding over your heart's door, do not resist Him. Open your heart to the touch of God. There is a resisting of and a *"striving against sin"* that leads even *"to bloodshed"* (Hebrews 12:4), and there is also a resisting of the Holy Spirit that will drive you into sin.

Stephen spoke with remarkable wisdom. Where he was, things began to move. You will find that there is always a moving when the Holy Spirit has control. These people were brought under conviction by the message of Stephen, but they resisted; they did anything and everything to stifle that conviction. Not only did they lie, but they got others to lie against this man, who would have laid down his life for any one of them. Stephen had been used by God to heal the sick and to perform miracles, yet they brought false accusations against him. What effect did their accusations have on Stephen? *"And all who sat in the council, looking steadfastly at him, saw his face as the face of an angel"* (Acts 6:15).

Something had happened in the life of this man chosen for menial service, and he had become mighty for God. How was it accomplished in him? It was because his aim was high. Faithful in little, Stephen was brought by God to full fruition. Under the inspiration of divine power, by which he spoke, his opponents could not help but listen. Even the angels listened, for he spoke with holy, prophetic utterance before that council. Beginning with Abraham and Moses, he continued unfolding the truth. What a marvelous exhortation! Take your Bibles and read the seventh chapter of Acts; "listen in" as the angels listened in. As light upon light, truth upon truth, revelation upon revelation found its way into his opponents' calloused hearts; they gazed at Stephen in astonishment. Perhaps their hearts became warm at times, and they may have said, "Truly, this man is sent by God." But then he hurled at them the truth:

> You stiffnecked and uncircumcised in heart and ears! You always resist the Holy Spirit; as your fathers did, so do you. Which of the prophets did your fathers not persecute? And they killed those who foretold the coming of the Just One, of whom you now have become the betrayers and murderers, who have received the law by the direction of angels and have not kept it. (Acts 7:51–53)

Then what happened? These men were moved; they were "cut to the heart, and they gnashed at him with their teeth" (verse 54).

There are two marvelous occasions in the Scriptures where the people were *"cut to the heart."* In the second chapter of the Acts of the Apostles, in the thirty-seventh verse, after Peter had delivered that inspired sermon on the Day of Pentecost, the people were *"cut to the heart"* with conviction, and three thousand souls were added to the church.

> Friends, it is worth dying a thousand deaths to gain that same fullness of the Holy Spirit as Stephen had!

Then, here is Stephen, speaking under the inspiration of the Holy Spirit, and the men of this council, being *"cut to the heart,"* rose up as one man to slay him. As you go down through this seventh chapter of Acts, starting with the fifty-fifth verse, what a picture you have before you! As I close my eyes, I can get a vision of this scene in every detail—the howling mob with their revengeful, murderous spirit, ready to devour this holy man, and he, *"being full of the Holy Spirit"* (verse 55), gazing steadfastly into heaven. What did he see there? From his place of helplessness, he looked up and said, *"Look! I see the heavens opened and the Son of Man standing at the right hand of God!"* (verse 56, emphasis added).

Is that the position that Jesus went to heaven to take? No! He went to sit at the right hand of the Father. But on behalf of the first martyr, on behalf of the man with that burning flame of Holy Spirit power, God's Son stood up in honorary testimony of him who was first called to serve tables and was faithful unto death.

But is that all? No! I am so glad that that is not all. As the stones came flying at Stephen, pounding his body, crashing into his bones, striking his head, mangling his beautiful face, what happened? How did this scene end? With a sublime, upward look, this man, chosen for an ordinary task but filled with the Holy Spirit, was so moved upon by God that he finished his earthly work in a blaze of glory, magnifying God with his last breath. Looking up into the face of the Master, he said, *"'Lord, do not charge them with this sin'. And when he had said this, he fell asleep"* (Acts 7:60).

Friends, it is worth dying a thousand deaths to gain that spirit. What a divine ending to the life and testimony of a man who had been chosen to serve tables.

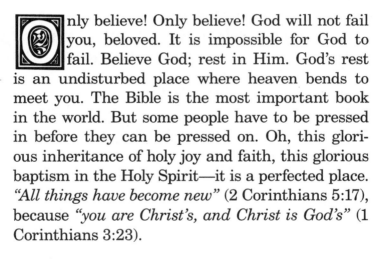

three

The Clothing of the Spirit for the World's Need

nly believe! Only believe! God will not fail you, beloved. It is impossible for God to fail. Believe God; rest in Him. God's rest is an undisturbed place where heaven bends to meet you. The Bible is the most important book in the world. But some people have to be pressed in before they can be pressed on. Oh, this glorious inheritance of holy joy and faith, this glorious baptism in the Holy Spirit—it is a perfected place. *"All things have become new"* (2 Corinthians 5:17), because *"you are Christ's, and Christ is God's"* (1 Corinthians 3:23).

> *But you shall receive power when the Holy Spirit has come upon you; and you shall be witnesses to Me in Jerusalem, and in all Judea and Samaria, and to the end of the earth.* (Acts 1:8)

God intends for us to walk in this royal way. When God opens a door, no man can shut it. (See Revelation 3:8.) John made a royal way, and

The Clothing of the Spirit

Jesus walked in it. Jesus left us the responsibility of allowing Him to bring forth through us the greater works. (See John 14:12.) Jesus left His disciples with much and with much more to be added until God receives us in that day.

When we receive power, we must stir ourselves up with the truth that we are responsible for the need around us. God will supply all our need (see Philippians 4:19) so that the need of the needy may be met through us. God has given us a great indwelling force of power. If we do not step into our privileges, it is a tragedy.

An Interpretation of Tongues:
God, who ravishes you, brings forth within the heart new revelation. We are changed by the Spirit from vision to vision, and glory to glory.

There is no standing still. *"As He is, so are we in this world"* (1 John 4:17). *"We are the offspring of God"* (Acts 17:29), and we have divine impulses. We must get into line. The life of the Son of God is to make the whole body aflame with fire. After we have received, we will have power. God has given me a blessed ministry by helping me to stir others up. The purpose of our gathering together must be for increase. I am zealous and eager that we come into the divine plan. If we wait for power, we have mistaken the position. We have been saying, "If only I could feel the power!"

We have been focusing too much on feeling the power. God is waiting for us to act. Jesus lived a life of perfect activity. He lived in the realm of divine appointment.

The pure in heart see God. (See Matthew 5:8.) Our *"God is a consuming fire"* (Deuteronomy 4:24). We must dare to press on until God comes forth in mighty power. May God give us the hearing of faith so that the power may come down like a cloud.

When I was at Stavanger in Norway, God told me to ask. He said, "I will give you every soul." It seemed too much! The voice came again: "Ask!" I dared to ask, and the power of God swept through the meeting like a mighty wind. We want this power in our cities. *"Go...and speak...all the words of this life"* (Acts 5:20). Press on until Jesus is glorified and multitudes are gathered in.

four

Called to
Serve

We are a very wealthy and privileged people to be able to gather together to worship the Lord. I count it a very holy thing to gather together to think of Him, because it is impossible to think of Him and be in any way unholy. The very thought of Jesus will confirm truth and righteousness and power in your mortal body. There is something very remarkable about Him. When John saw Him, the impression that he had was that He was the *"lamb without blemish and without spot"* (1 Peter 1:19). When God speaks about Jesus, He says, *"He came forth in the brightness of the expression of the countenance of God."* When revelation comes, it says, *"In Him dwells all the fullness"* (Colossians 2:9).

His character is beautiful. His display of meekness is lovely. His compassion is greater than that of anyone in all of humanity. He felt infirmities. He helps those who pass through trials. And it is to be said about Him what is not said about anyone else: "[He] *was in all points tempted as we are, yet without sin*" (Hebrews 4:15).

I want you, as the author of Hebrews wonderfully said, to *"consider Him who endured such hostility from sinners against Himself, lest you become weary and discouraged in your souls"* (Hebrews 12:3). When you are weary and tempted and tried and all men are against you, consider Him who has passed through it all, so that He might be able to help you in the trial as you are passing through it. He will sustain you in the strife. When all things seem to indicate that you have failed, the Lord of Hosts, the God of Jacob, the salvation of our Christ will so reinforce you that you will be stronger than any concrete building that was ever made.

An Interpretation of Tongues:

Your God, your Lord, in whom you trust, will make you so strong in the Lord and in the power of His might that no evil thing will befall you. As He was with Moses, He will be with you. As He stood by Daniel, He will cause the lions' mouths to close. He will shut up all that is against you; and the favor of heaven, the smile of the Most High, the kiss of His love, will make you know you are covered with the Dove.

Called to Serve

Our Calling

The following Scripture is so beautiful: *"I, therefore, the prisoner of the Lord, beseech you to walk worthy of the calling with which you were called"* (Ephesians 4:1).

Paul, who spoke to us in this verse, was an example for the church. He was filled with the loveliness of the character of the Master through the Spirit's power. He was zealous that we may walk worthy. This is the day of calling that he spoke about; this is the opportunity of our lifetime. This is the place where God increases strength or opens the door of a new way of ministry so that we will come into like-mindedness with this holy apostle who was a prisoner.

Lowliness and Meekness

The passage goes on to say, *"With all lowliness and gentleness, with longsuffering, bearing with one another in love"* (Ephesians 4:2).

Jesus emphasized the new commandment when He left us: *"A new commandment I give to you, that you love one another; as I have loved you, that you also love one another"* (John 13:34). To the extent that we miss this instruction, we miss all the Master's instruction. If we miss that commandment, we miss everything. All the future summits of glory are yours in the very fact that you have been recreated in a deeper order by that commandment He gave us.

When we reach this attitude of love, then we make no mistake about lowliness. We will submit ourselves in the future in order that we may be useful to one another. The greatest plan that Jesus ever presented in His ministry was the ministry of service. He said, *"I am among you as the One who serves"* (Luke 22:27). And when we come to a place where we serve for pure love's sake, because it is the divine hand of the Master upon us, we will find out that we will never fail. Love never fails when it is divinely appointed in us. However, the so-called love in our human nature does fail and has failed from the beginning.

> The greatest plan that Jesus ever presented in His ministry was the ministry of service.

Suppose a man corresponds with me, seeking to learn more about me and to establish a relationship. The only thing I would have to say in answering his letters is, "Brother, all that I know about Wigglesworth is bad." There is no good thing in human nature. However, all that I know about the new creation in Wigglesworth is good. The important thing is whether we are living in the old creation or the new creation.

So I implore you to see that there is a lowliness, a humbleness, that leads you to meekness, that leads you to separate yourself from the world, that puts you so in touch with the Master that you know you are touching God. The blood of Jesus cleanses you from sin and all pollution. (See 1 John 1:7.) There is something in this holy position that makes you know you are free from the power of the Enemy.

We have yet to see the forcefulness of the Word of God. I refer to it in passing, as described in Hebrews:

> *For the word of God is living and powerful, and sharper than any two-edged sword, piercing even to the division of soul and spirit, and of joints and marrow, and is a discerner of the thoughts and intents of the heart.* (Hebrews 4:12)

The Word, the life, the presence, the power, is in your body, in the very marrow of your bones, and absolutely everything else must be discharged. Sometimes we do not fully reflect on this wonderful truth: the Word, the life, the Christ who is the Word, separates your soul from your spirit. What a wonderful work! The Spirit divides you from soul affection, from human weakness, from all depravity. The blood of Jesus can cleanse your blood until your very soul is purified and your very nature is destroyed by the nature of the living Christ.

I am speaking to you about resurrection touches. In Christ, we have encountered divine resurrection touches. In the greatest work God ever did on the face of the earth, He had to use His operation power: Christ was raised from the dead by the operation of the power of God. As the resurrection of Christ operates in our hearts, it will dethrone the wrong things. And at the same time that it dethrones, it will build the right things. Callousness will have to change; hardness will have to disappear; all evil thoughts will have to go. And in the place of these will be lowliness of mind.

What beautiful cooperation with God in thought and power and holiness! The Master *"made Himself of no reputation"* (Philippians 2:7). He absolutely left the glory of heaven, with all its wonder. He left it and submitted Himself to humiliation. He went down, down, down into death for one purpose only: that He might destroy the power of death, even the Devil, and deliver those people who all their lifetime have been subject to fear—deliver them from the fear of death and the Devil. (See Hebrews 2:14–15.)

This is a wonderful plan for us. But how will it come to pass? By transformation, resurrection, thoughts of holiness, intense zeal, desire for all of God, until we live and move in the atmosphere of holiness.

If I say "holiness" or "baptism" or "resurrection" or "rapture," remember that all these words are tremendous. And there is another phrase I

would like to emphasize: *"After you were illumi-
nated"* (Hebrews 10:32). Have you been to the
place of illumination? What does the word mean?
Illumination means this: that your very mind,
which was depraved, is now the mind of Christ;
the very nature that was bound now has a resurrection touch; your very body has come in contact
with the life of God until you who were lost are
found, and you who were
dead are alive again by
the resurrection power
of the Word of the life of
Christ. What a glorious
inheritance in the Spirit!

> Resurrection
> life means living
> in the Spirit,
> wakened into all
> likeness, made
> alive by the
> same Spirit!

Have you come to
this place? Don't forget
the ladder that Jacob saw.
(See Genesis 28:10–22.)
As I was nearing Jerusalem and saw the city for
the first time, someone said to me, "See that place
there? That is where Jacob saw the ladder that
reached from earth to heaven."

Believer, if you have not reached all this, the
ladder extends from heaven to earth to take you
from earth to heaven. Do not be afraid of taking
the steps. You will not slip back. Have faith in God.
Experience divine resurrection life—more divine
in thought, more wonderful in revelation. Resurrection life means living in the Spirit, wakened
into all likeness, made alive by the same Spirit!

An Interpretation of Tongues:

He rose, and in His rising, He lifted us and He placed us in the place of seating, and then gave us a holy language, and then began to entertain us and show in us that now the body is His and that we become members in particular of the body. Sometimes He chastens us so that all the dross might go and all the wood and the stubble might be burned in the testing, so that He might get purer gold, purer life, purer soul, so that there should be nothing in the body that should be defiling, but He should take us out of the world and make us like a ripe shock of corn, ready for the dawning of the morning.

Are you lowly and meek in your mind? It is the divine plan of the Savior. You must be like Him. Do you desire to be like Him? There is nothing but yourself that can hinder you in this. You are the one who stops the current. You are the one who stops the life. The river and the current are coming just now; I feel them all over me.

While ministering in one place, we had a banquet for people who were distressed—people who were lame and weary, blind and diseased in every way. We had a big crowd of people, and we fed them all.

After we got them well filled with all the good things that were provided, we said, "Now we are going to give you some entertainment."

Called to Serve

A man who had spent many years in a wheel-chair but had been healed came onto the platform and told how he had been set free. A person who had suffered from a hemorrhage for many years came and testified. A blind man came and told how his eyes had been opened. For one hour, the people were entertained.

Then I said to the people, "Are you ready?"

Oh, they were all so ready! A dear man got hold of a boy who was encased in iron from top to bottom, lifted him up, and placed him onto the platform. Hands were laid upon him in the name of Jesus.

"Papa! Papa! Papa!" the boy said. "It's going all over me! Oh, Papa, come and take these irons off!" I do like to hear children speak; they say such wonderful things. The father took the irons off, and the life of God had gone all over the boy!

This is what I feel: the life of God going all over me, the power of God all over me. Don't you know this is the resurrection touch? This is the divine life; this is what God has brought us into. Let it go over us, Lord—the power of the Holy Spirit, the resurrection of heaven, the sweetness of Your blessing, the joy of the Lord!

If our fellowship below with Jesus be so sweet,
What heights of rapture shall we know
When round His throne we meet!

An Interpretation of Tongues:
The Spirit sweetly falls like the dew, just as
still on the grass, and as it comes, it is for
a purpose—God's purpose. It may be withered grass, but God calls it to come forth
again. And the Spirit of the Lord is right
in the midst of you this morning. Though
you might have been withered, dried, and
barren for a long time, the dew is falling.
God is in the midst of us with His spirit
of revival, and He is saying to you, "All
things are possible; only believe," and He
will change you.

THE UNITY OF THE SPIRIT

*"Endeavoring to keep the unity of the Spirit in
the bond of peace"* (Ephesians 4:3).

You are bound forever out of loyalty to God to
see that no division comes into the church body,
to see that nothing comes into the assembly, as it
came into David's flock, to tear and rend the body.
You have to be careful. If a person comes along
with a prophecy and you find that it is tearing
down and bringing trouble, denounce it accord-
ingly; judge it by the Word. You will find that all
true prophecy will be perfectly full of hopeful-
ness. It will have compassion; it will have comfort; it will have edification. So if anything comes
into the church that you know is hurting the flock
and disturbing the assembly, you must see to it

that you begin to pray so that this thing is put to death. Bring unity in the bonds of perfection so that the church of God will receive edification. Then the church will begin to be built up in the faith and the establishing of truth, and believers will be one.

Do not forget that God means for us to be very faithful to the church so that we do not allow anything to come into the church to break up the body. You cannot find anything in the body in its relation to Christ that has schism in it. Christ's life in the body—there is no schism in that. When Christ's life comes into the church, there will be no discord; there will be a perfect blending of heart and hand, and it will be lovely. Endeavor *"to keep the unity of the Spirit in the bond of peace"* (Ephesians 4:3).

ONE BODY

Now I come to a very important point: *"There is one body"* (verse 4).

There is one body. Recognize that fact. When schism comes into the body, believers always act as though there were more than one. For instance, there is the Wesleyan Church, there is the Baptist Church, and there are many other churches. What do I need to notice about them? I have to see that right in that body, right in that church, God has a remnant belonging to His body. All the members of that church may not be of the body, but God has a remnant in that church. I should not go out and denounce the Baptists, the Wesleyans, or any other church. What I need to do, what I must do, is to so live in the Spirit of Christ that they will see that I am one with them. It is the Holy Spirit in the new church, in the body, the spiritual body, who is uniting, binding, and mightily moving. In every church, whether that church baptizes or not, there is a place where the Spirit is.

Now, beloved, the baptism of the Spirit is to be planted deeper and deeper in us until there is not a part that is left, and the manifestation of the power of the new creation by the Holy Spirit is right in our mortal bodies. Where we once were, He now reigns supreme, manifesting the very Christ inside of us, the Holy Spirit fulfilling all things right there.

> In every church, whether that church baptizes or not, there is a place where the Spirit is.

Jesus has been wonderfully ordained; He has been incarnated by God, and God has given Him preeminence. He has to be preeminent in us. And someday we will see the preeminence of this wonderful Savior, and we will take our crowns and place them at His feet. Then He will put the Father in all preeminence and will take all our crowns and us also and present us to the Father, with Himself, so that the Father will be all in all, forever and ever.

That will take ten million years. In thinking about it, my calculation is that the Marriage and the Supper of the Lamb will take fifty million years. "What do you mean?" you ask. *"With the Lord one day is as a thousand years"* (2 Peter 3:8). Our supernatural bodies, in the glory of their infinite relationship, will so live in the bliss of heaven that time will fly. The Supper and the Marriage will be supremely delightful and full and refreshing, pure and glorious and light. Oh, hallelujah! It is coming! It is not past; it is on the way. It is a glory we have yet to enter into.

One Lord and One Faith

There is one body and one Spirit, just as you were called in one hope of your calling; one Lord, one faith, one baptism.

(Ephesians 4:4–5)

"One Lord." Oh, it is lovely! One Lord, one heart, one love, one association. *"One Lord, one faith, one baptism."* It is the baptism of the Spirit, the baptism of the new creation order, the baptism into divine life, the baptism with fire, the baptism with zeal, the baptism with passion, the baptism with inward travail. Oh, it is a baptism indeed! Jesus had it. He travailed; He acted with compassion.

"One Lord." We are all one, all in Christ Jesus, all one in Christ. We have *"one faith,"* which lays hold of the immensities, which dares to believe, which holds fast to what we have, so that no one may take our crowns. (See Revelation 3:11.) For we are being quickened by this resurrection, and now faith lays hold.

Contend for eternal life. Lay hold of it—eternal life! It is something we cannot handle, something we cannot see, yet it is more real than we are. Lay hold of it. Let no man rob you of it. It is a crown; it is a position in the Holy One. It is a place of identification. It is a place of Him bringing you into order. Only He can do it—and He does it.

THE GOD WHO IS OVER ALL

Let us look at the next verse, which is very beautiful, for here is our position in this world: *"One God and Father of all, who is above all, and through all, and in you all"* (Ephesians 4:6).

"Who is above all." Think of that! It does not matter what the Enemy may bring to you, or try to bring; remember, the Father, who is above all, is over you. Is there anything else? Yes, the next thought is larger still: *"Through all."* And the next: *"In you all."* The God of power, majesty, and glory can bring you to a place of dethroning everything else! The Father of all is *"above all, and through all, and in you all."*

Called to Serve

Do you dare to believe it? You should go away with such inspiration in the area of faith that you will never have a doubt again, and I want above all things to take you to that place.

Remember, God our Father is so intensely desirous to have all the fullness of the manifestation of His power, that we do not have to have one thing that His Son did not come to bring. We have to have perfect redemption; we have to know all the powers of righteousness; we have to understand perfectly that we are brought to the place where He is with us in all power, dethroning the power of the Enemy.

God over you—that is real. The God who is over you is more than a million times greater than the Devil, than the powers of evil, than the powers of darkness. How do I know? Hear what the Devil said to God about Job: *"Have You not made a hedge around him?"* (Job 1:10). This verse means that the Devil was unable to get near Job because there was a hedge. What was the hedge? It was the almighty power of God. It was not a thorny hedge; it was not a hedge of thistles. It was the presence of the Lord all around Job. And the presence of the Lord Almighty is so around us that the Devil cannot break through that wonderful covering.

The Devil is against the living Christ and wants to destroy Him, and if you are filled with the living Christ, the Devil is eager to get you out of the way in order to destroy Christ's power. Say this to the Lord: "Now, Lord, look after this property of yours." Then the Devil cannot get near you. When does he get near? When you dethrone Christ, ignoring His rightful position over you, in you, and through you.

You will be strong if you believe this truth. I preach faith, and I know it will carry you through if you dare to believe. Faith is the victory—always. Glory to Jesus!

THE GIFTS OF CHRIST

Notice next that the apostle Paul received revelation about Jesus. He spoke about the grace and the gifts of Christ—not the gifts of the Holy Spirit, but the gifts of Christ: *"But to each one of us grace was given according to the measure of Christ's gift"* (Ephesians 4:7).

The gifts of Christ are so different from the gifts of the Holy Spirit that I want to explain this for a moment:

> *Therefore He says, "When He ascended on high, He led captivity captive, and gave gifts to men."...And He Himself gave some to be apostles, some prophets, some evangelists, and some pastors and teachers, for the equipping of the saints for the work of ministry, for the edifying of the body of Christ.* (Ephesians 4:8, 11–12)

These verses are in the Epistles. The Gospels are the gospel of the kingdom. In the Acts of the Apostles, those who believed repented, were saved, were baptized, and became eligible to come into the Epistles, so that they might be in the body as is described in the Epistles. The body is not made up after you get into the Epistles; you are joined to the body the moment you believe.

For instance, some of you may have children, and they have different names, but the moment they appeared in the world, they were in your family. The moment they were born, they became a part of your family.

> The moment you are born of God, you are in the family, and you are in the body collectively and particularly.

The moment you are born of God, you are in the family, and you are in the body, as He is in the body, and you are in the body collectively and particularly. After you come into the body, then the body has to receive the sealing of the promise, or the fulfillment of promise, that is, that Christ will be in you, reigning in you mightily. The Holy Spirit will come to unveil the King in all His glory so that He might reign as King there, the Holy Spirit serving in every way to make Him King.

You are in the body. The Holy Spirit gives gifts in the body. Living in this holy order, you may find that revelation comes to you and makes you a prophet. Some of you may have a clear understanding that you have been called into apostleship. Some of you may have perfect knowledge that you are to be pastors. When you come to be sealed with the Spirit of promise, then you find out that Jesus is pleased and gives gifts, in order that the church might come into a perfect position of being so blended together that there could be no division. Jesus wants His church to be a perfect body—perfect in stature, perfect in oneness in Him.

I have been speaking to this end: that you may see the calling that Paul was speaking about—humility of mind, meekness of spirit, knowing that God is in you and through you, knowing that the power of the Spirit is mightily bringing you to the place where not only the gifts of the Spirit but also the gifts of Christ have been given to you, making you eligible for the great work you have to do.

My purpose in this teaching was not to tell what God has for you in the future. Press in now, and claim your rights. Let the Lord Jesus be so glorified that He will make you fruit-bearers—strong in power, giving glory to God, having *"no confidence in the flesh"* (Philippians 3:3) but being separated from natural things, now in the Spirit, living fully in the will of God.

five

The Cry of the Spirit

ohn the Baptist said, *"I am 'The voice of one crying in the wilderness: "Make straight the way of the Lord,"'* as the prophet Isaiah said"* (John 1:23). He also said, *"Repent, for the kingdom of heaven is at hand!"* (Matthew 3:2). *"Then Jerusalem, all Judea, and all the region around the Jordan went out to him and were baptized by him in the Jordan, confessing their sins"* (verses 5–6).

John's clothing was camel's hair, his belt leather, his food locusts and wild honey. (See verse 4.) No angels or shepherds or wise men or stars heralded John's birth. But the heavenly messenger Gabriel, who had spoken to Daniel and to Mary, also spoke to John's father, Zacharias.

In the wilderness, John was without the food and clothing of his earthly father's priestly home. He had only a groan, a cry—the cry of the Spirit. Yet from John's place in the wilderness, he moved the whole land. God cried through him. It was the cry of the Spirit—oh, that awful cry. All the land was moved by that piercing cry.

Some are ashamed to cry. There is loneliness in a cry. However, God is with a person who has only a cry.

WATER BAPTISM

So God spoke to John and told him about a new thing—water baptism.

> *And John bore witness, saying, "I saw the Spirit descending from heaven like a dove, and He remained upon Him. I did not know Him, but He who sent me to baptize with water said to me, 'Upon whom you see the Spirit descending, and remaining on Him, this is He who baptizes with the Holy Spirit.' And I have seen and testified that this is the Son of God."*
>
> (John 1:32–34)

God spoke to John in the wilderness about water baptism. It was a clean cut; it was a new way. He had been with those of the circumcision; now he was an outcast. It was the breaking down of the old plan.

REPENTANCE

The people heard his cry—oh, that cry, the awful cry of the Spirit—and the message that he gave: *"Repent, for the kingdom of heaven is at* hand!' (Matthew 3:2). Make straight paths—no treading down of others or exacting undue rights. *'Make straight paths for your feet'* (Hebrews 12:13)." All were startled! All were awakened! They thought the Messiah had come. The searching was tremendous! Is this He? Who can it be? John said, "I am a voice, crying, crying, making a way for the Messiah to come."

> *Now this is the testimony of John, when the Jews sent priests and Levites from Jerusalem to ask him, "Who are you?" He confessed, and did not deny, but confessed, "I am not the Christ." And they asked him, "What then? Are you Elijah?" He said, "I am not." "Are you the Prophet?" And he answered, "No."...He said: "I am 'The voice of one crying in the wilderness: "Make straight the way of the LORD,"'" as the prophet Isaiah said."*
>
> (John 1:19–21, 23)

Individuals were purged; they found purpose. God pressed life through John. Through him, God moved multitudes and changed the situation. The banks of the Jordan were covered with people. The conviction was tremendous. They cried out. The prophet Isaiah had predicted, *"The rough ways* [will be made] *smooth; and all flesh shall see the salvation of God"* (Luke 3:5–6).

> *Then he* [John] *said to the multitudes that came out to be baptized by him, "Brood of*

> *vipers! Who warned you to flee from the wrath to come? Therefore bear fruits worthy of repentance, and do not begin to say to yourselves, 'We have Abraham as our father.' For I say to you that God is able to raise up children to Abraham from these stones. And even now the ax is laid to the root of the trees. Therefore every tree which does not bear good fruit is cut down and thrown into the fire." So the people asked him, saying, "What shall we do then?" He answered and said to them, "He who has two tunics, let him give to him who has none; and he who has food, let him do likewise." Then tax collectors also came to be baptized, and said to him, "Teacher, what shall we do?" And he said to them, "Collect no more than what is appointed for you." Likewise the soldiers asked him, saying, "And what shall we do?" So he said to them, "Do not intimidate anyone or accuse falsely, and be content with your wages."* (Luke 3:7–14)

The people, the multitude, cried out and were baptized by John in the Jordan, confessing their sins.

ALONE WITH GOD

Oh, to be alone with God. God's Word came to John when he was alone.

The Cry of the Spirit

The word of God came to John the son of Zacharias in the wilderness. And he went... preaching a baptism of repentance for the remission of sins. (Luke 3:2–3)

Alone! Alone!
  Jesus bore it all alone!
He gave Himself to save His own.
  He suffered—bled and died alone—alone.

Oh, to be alone with God, to get His mind, His thoughts, and His impression and revelation of the need of the people.

There was nothing ordinary about John—all was extraordinary. Herod was reproved by him because of Herodias, his brother Philip's wife, and for all the evils that Herod had done. Herodias's daughter danced before Herod, who promised her up to half his kingdom. She asked for John the Baptist's head.

This holy man was alone. God had John in such a way that he could express that cry—the burden for the whole land. He could cry for the sins of the people.

A Call to God's People to Cry

God is holy. We are the children of Abraham—the children of faith. Awful judgment is coming. Cry! Cry!

John could not help but cry because of the people's sin. John had been filled with the Holy

Spirit from his mother's womb. (See Luke 1:15.) He had the burden. He was stern, but through his work, the land was open to Jesus. Jesus walked in the way; He came a new way.

"John came neither eating nor drinking" (Matthew 11:18)—John came crying. The only place he could breathe and be free was in the wilderness—the atmosphere of heaven—until he turned with a message to declare the preparation needed. Before Jesus came, repentance came to open up the place of redemption.

First, there must be a working of the Spirit in you; then God will work through you for others.

John's father and mother were left behind. His heart bled at the altar. He bore the burden, the cry, and the need of the people.

An Interpretation of Tongues:
Give way unto the Lord, even to the operation of the Spirit. A people known of God, doing exploits, gripped by God. Continue in the things revealed unto you. The enemy put to flight. Even those around you will acknowledge that the Lord has blessed.

six

Experiences Worked Out by Humility

What a privilege to care for the flock of God, to be used by God to encourage the people, to help stand against the many trials that affect the needy. What a holy calling! We each have our own work, and we must do it, so that boldness may be ours in the day of the Master's appearing, and so that no man can take our crowns. (See Revelation 3:11.) Since the Lord is always encouraging us, we have encouragement for others. We must have a willingness, a ready mind, a yielding to the mind of the Spirit. There is no place for the child of God in God's great plan except in humility.

THE PLACE OF KNOWING OUR NEED

God can never do all He wants to do, all that He came to do through the Word, until He gets us to the place where He can trust us, and where we are in abiding fellowship with Him in His great plan for the world's redemption. We have this truth illustrated in the life of Jacob. It took God twenty-one years to bring Jacob to the place of humility, contrition of heart, and brokenness of spirit. God even gave him power to wrestle with strength, and Jacob said, "I think I can manage after all," until God touched his thigh, making him know that he was mortal and that he was dealing with immortality. As long as we think we can save ourselves, we will try to do it.

In Mark 5:25–34, we have the story of the woman who had suffered many things from many physicians and had spent all that she had. She was no better but rather grew worse. She said, *"If only I may touch His clothes, I shall be made well"* (verse 28). She came to know her need. Our full cupboard is often our greatest hindrance. It is when we are empty and undone, when we come to God in our nothingness and helplessness, that He picks us up.

PETER'S WORDS OF WISDOM

Let's take a look at the fifth chapter of 1 Peter. Peter said, *"Therefore humble yourselves under the mighty hand of God, that He may exalt you in due time"* (verse 6). Look at the Master at the Jordan River, submitting Himself to the baptism of John, then again submitting Himself to the cruel Cross. Truly, angels desire to look into these things (see 1 Peter 1:12), and all heaven is waiting for the man who will burn all the bridges behind him and allow God to begin a plan in righteousness, so full, so sublime, beyond all human thought, but according to the revelation of the Spirit.

"Casting all your care upon Him, for He cares for you" (1 Peter 5:7). He cares! We sometimes forget this. If we descend into the natural, all goes wrong, but when we trust Him, how blessed it is. Many times I have experienced my helplessness and nothingness, and casting my care upon Him has proved that He cares.

Verse eight tells us to *"be sober, be vigilant."* What does it mean to be sober? It means to have a clear knowledge that we are powerless to manage, but also to have a rest of faith, knowing that God is close at hand to deliver all

> It is when we are empty and undone, when we come to God in our nothingness and helplessness, that He picks us up.

the time. The Adversary's opportunity is when we think that we are something and try to open our own door. Our thoughts, words, and deeds must all be in the power of the Holy Spirit. Oh yes, we need to be sober—not only sober, but vigilant. We need not only to be filled with the Spirit but also to have a *"go forth"* in us, a knowledge that God's holy presence is with us. To be sober and vigilant, to have an ability to judge, discern, and balance things that differ—this is what we need.

*Your adversary the devil walks about like a
roaring lion, seeking whom he may devour.
Resist him, steadfast in the faith.*

(1 Peter 5:8–9)

We must resist in the hour when Satan's
schemes may bewilder us, when we are almost
swept off our feet, and when darkness is upon us
to such a degree that it seems as if some evil thing
had overtaken us. *"Resist him, steadfast in the
faith." "He who keeps Israel shall neither slum-
ber nor sleep"* (Psalm 121:4). God covers us, for no
human can stand against the powers of hell.

An Interpretation of Tongues:
The strongholds of God are stronger than
the strength of man, and He never fails to
interpose on behalf of His own.

"After you have suffered a while" (1 Peter
5:10). Then there is some suffering? Yes! But it is
*"not worthy to be compared with the glory which
shall be revealed in us"* (Romans 8:18). The difference is so great that our suffering is not even
worthy of mention. Ours is an eternal glory, from
glory to glory, until we are swallowed up, until we
are swallowed up in Him, the Lord of glory.

FOUR HELPS FOR THE HEART

Then, also in 1 Peter 5:10, we have four other
things that enable the heart to be fixed in God:
*"But may the God of all grace, who called us to
His eternal glory by Christ Jesus, after you have*

suffered a while, perfect, establish, strengthen, and settle you." The God of all grace wants to do the following in us: first, *"perfect"*; second, *"establish"*; third, *"strengthen"*; and fourth, *"settle."*

First is *"perfect."* In the book of Hebrews, we read,

> *May the God of peace...make you complete [*"perfect," KJV*] in every good work to do His will, working in you what is well pleasing in His sight, through Jesus Christ.*
> (Hebrews 13:20–21)

Keep in mind that when perfection is spoken of in the Word, it is always through a joining up with eternal things. Perfection is a working in us of the will of God.

There are some of us who would be fainthearted if we thought we had to be perfect to receive the blessing of God. We would ask ourselves, "How is it going to happen?" However, we find as we continue to follow God that the purpose of eternal life is advancement, for we are saved by the blood. Our actions, our minds, are covered by the blood of Jesus, and as we yield and yield, we find ourselves in possession of another mind, even the mind of Christ (see 1 Corinthians 2:16), which causes us to understand the perfection of His will.

Someone may be saying, "I can never be perfect! It is beyond my greatest thought." You're right; it is! But as we press on, the Holy Spirit enlightens, and we enter in, as Paul said, according to the revelation of the Spirit. I am perfected as I launch out into God by faith, His precious blood covering my sin, His righteousness covering my unrighteousness, His perfection covering my imperfection. This is a very important fact: I am holy and perfect in Him.

Second is *"establish."* You must be established in the fact that it is His life, not yours. You must have faith in His Word, faith in His life. You are supplanted by Another. You are disconnected from the earth. You are insulated by faith.

Third is *"strengthen."* You are strengthened by the fact that God is doing the business, not you. You are in the plan that God is working out.

An Interpretation of Tongues:
There is nothing in itself that can bring out that which God designs. What God intends is always a going on to perfection until we are like unto Him. It is an establishment of righteousness on His own Word.

Fourth is *"settle."* What does it mean to be settled? It means knowing that I am in union with His will, that I am established in the knowledge of it, that day by day, I am strengthened. It is an eternal work of righteousness, until by the Spirit we are perfected. First is an enduring, then an establishing, a strengthening, and a settling.

This happens according to our faith. It happens as we believe.

Now a closing word: *"To Him be the glory and the dominion forever and ever"* (1 Peter 5:11). How can this verse be realized in my case? By living for His glory. There must be no withdrawal, no relinquishing, no looking back, but going on, on, on, for His glory now and forever. We must go on until, like Enoch, we walk with God and are not, for God has taken us. (See Genesis 5:24.)

seven

The Flood Tide

"The increase of God."
—Colossians 2:19 KJV

Wherever Jesus went, the multitudes followed Him, because He lived, moved, breathed, was swallowed up, clothed, and filled by God. He was God; and as the Son of Man, the Spirit of God—the Spirit of creative holiness—rested upon Him. It is lovely to be holy. Jesus came to impart to us the Spirit of holiness.

We are only at the edge of things; the almighty plan for the future is marvelous. God must do something to increase. We need a revival to revive all we touch within us and outside of us. We need a flood tide with a deluge behind it. Jesus left one hundred twenty men to turn the world upside down. The Spirit is upon us to change our situation. We must move on; we must let God increase in us for the deliverance of multitudes; and we must travail until souls are born and quickened into a new relationship with heaven. Jesus had divine authority with power, and He left it for us. We must preach truth, holiness, and purity *"in the inward parts"* (Psalm 51:6).

> *You have loved righteousness and hated lawlessness; therefore God, Your God, has anointed You with the oil of gladness more than Your companions.* (Hebrews 1:9)

I am thirsty for more of God. He was not only holy, but He loved holiness.

An Interpretation of Tongues:

It is the depths that God gets into that we may reflect Him and manifest a life having Christ enthroned in the heart, drinking into a new fullness, new intuition, for as He is, so are we in this world.

Jesus trod the winepress alone (see Isaiah 63:3), despising the cross and the shame. He bore it all alone so that we might be *"partakers of the divine nature"* (2 Peter 1:4), sharers in the divine plan of holiness. That's revival—Jesus manifesting divine authority. He was without sin. People saw the Lamb of God in a new way. Hallelujah! Let us live in holiness, and revival will come down, and God will enable us to do the work to which we are appointed. All Jesus said came to pass: signs, wonders, mighty deeds. Only believe, and yield and yield, until all the vision is fulfilled.

A MIGHTY FAITH

God has a design, a purpose, a rest of faith. We are saved by faith and kept by faith. Faith is substance; it is also evidence. (See Hebrews 11:1.) God is! He is! And *"He is a rewarder of those who diligently seek Him"* (verse 6). We are to testify, to bear witness to what we know. To know that we know is a wonderful position to be in.

An Interpretation of Tongues:
The Lord is the great promoter of divine possibility, pressing you into the attitude of daring to believe all that the Word says. We are to be living words, epistles of Christ, known and read of all men. The revelation of Christ, past and future; in Him all things consist. He is in us.

We are living in the inheritance of faith because of the grace of God. We are saved for eternity by the operation of the Spirit, who brings forth unto God. Heaven is brought to earth until God quickens all things into beauty, manifesting His power in living witnesses. God is in us for the world, so that the world may be blessed. We need power to lay hold of Omnipotence and to impart to others the Word of Life. This is a new epoch with new vision and new power. Christ in us is greater than we know. All things are possible if you dare to believe. The treasure is in earthen vessels so that Jesus may be glorified. (See 2 Corinthians 4:7.)

Let us go forth bringing glory to God. Faith is substance, a mightiness of reality, a deposit of divine nature, the creative God within. The moment you believe, you are clothed with a new power to lay hold of possibility and make it reality. The people said to Jesus, *"Lord, give us this bread always"* (John 6:34). Jesus said, *"He who feeds on Me will live because of Me"* (verse 57).

Have the faith of God. The man who comes into great association with God needs a heavenly measure. Faith is the greatest of all. We are saved by a new life, the Word of God, an association with the living Christ. A new creation continually takes us into new revelation.

THE LIFE OF GOD WITHIN US

In the beginning was the Word, and the Word was with God, and the Word was God....All things were made through Him, and without Him nothing was made that was made. (John 1:1, 3)

All was made by the Word. I am begotten by His Word. There is a substance within me that has almighty power in it if I dare to believe. Faith goes on to be an act, a reality, a deposit of God, an almighty flame moving me to act, so that signs and wonders are manifested. I have a living faith within my earthen body.

Are you begotten? Is faith an act within you? Some need a touch; some are captives and need liberty. As many as Jesus touched were made perfectly whole. Faith takes you to the place where God reigns and you drink from His bountiful store. Unbelief is sin, for Jesus went to death to bring us the light of life.

Jesus asked, *"Are you able to drink the cup that I am about to drink, and be baptized with the baptism that I am baptized with?"* (Matthew 20:22). The cup and the baptism are a joined position. You cannot live if you want to bring everything into life. His life is manifested power overflowing. We must decrease if the life of God is to be manifested. (See John 3:30.) There is not room for two kinds of life in one body. Death for life—that is the price to pay for the manifested power of God through you. As you die to human desire, there comes a fellowship within, perfected cooperation, you ceasing, God increasing. God in you is a living substance, a spiritual nature. You live by another life, the faith of the Son of God.

> Faith takes you to the place where God reigns and you drink from His bountiful store.

An Interpretation of Tongues:
The Spirit, He breathed through and quickens until the body is a temple exhibiting

Jesus—His life, His freshness, a new life divine. Paul said, "Christ lives in me, and the life I live in the flesh I live by faith."

As the Holy Spirit reveals Jesus, He is real—the living Word, effective, acting, speaking, thinking, praying, and singing. Oh, it is a wonderful life, this substance of the Word of God, which includes possibility and opportunity. *"Greater is he that is in you"* (1 John 4:4 KJV). Paul said, *"When I am weak, then I am strong"* (2 Corinthians 12:10).

Jesus walked in supremacy; He lived in the kingdom. And God will take us through because of Calvary. He has given us power over all the power of the enemy. (See Luke 10:19.) He won it for us at Calvary. All must be subject to His power. What should we do to work the works? *"This is the work of God, that you believe"* (John 6:29). Whatsoever He says will come to pass. That is God's Word.

A frail, weak man with sunken cheeks said to me, "Can you help me?" Beloved, there is not one who cannot be helped. God has opened the doors for us to let Him manifest signs and wonders. The authority is inside, not outside.

Could I help him? He had been fed liquid food through a tube for three months. I said, "Go home and eat a good supper." He did, and woke up to find the tube hole closed up. God knew he did not need two holes to eat by.

We must remain in a strong, resolute resting on the authority of God's Word. We must have one great desire and purpose: to do what He says. We must live in this holy Word, rejoicing in the manifestation of the life of God on behalf of the sick and perishing multitudes. Amen.

eight

Changing Strengths to Save Another

Paul, *an apostle of Jesus Christ by the will of God"* (2 Corinthians 1:1). What a beautiful thought: we are here by the will of God. By the will of God, we are saved; by the will of God, we are sanctified; by the will of God, we are baptized in the Holy Spirit.

THE HOLY SPIRIT IS OUR COMFORTER

"Blessed be the God and Father of our Lord Jesus Christ, the Father of mercies and God of all comfort" (verse 3). Jesus could not have breathed any greater words than John 14:16: *"I will pray the Father, and He will give you another Helper ['Comforter,' KJV], that He may abide with you forever."*

"The Father of mercies and God of all comfort." We need a revelation of a greater power, an abiding presence sustaining and comforting us in the hour of trial, ready at a moment's notice, an inbreathing of God in the human life. What more

do we need in these last days when perilous times are upon us than to be filled, saturated, baptized with the Holy Spirit? Baptized. Baptized into Him, never to come out. How comforting! Exhilarating! Joyful! May it please the Lord to establish us in this state of grace. May we know nothing among men except Jesus Christ and Him crucified. (See 1 Corinthians 2:2.) May we be clothed with His Spirit—nothing outside of the blessed Holy Spirit. This, beloved, is God's ideal for us.

COMFORT IN THE MIDST OF TRIBULATION

[God] comforts us in all our tribulation, that we may be able to comfort those who are in any trouble, with the comfort with which we ourselves are comforted by God.
(2 Corinthians 1:4)

Are we here in this experience?

> Where He may lead me I will go,
> For I have learned to trust Him so,
> And I remember it was for me,
> That He was slain on Calvary.

"*[God] comforts us in all our tribulation!*" God has chosen me to go through certain experiences to profit others. In all ages, God has had His witnesses, and He is teaching, chastening, correcting, and moving me just up to the point that I am able to bear it, in order to meet a needy soul who would otherwise go down without such comfort.

Changing Strengths to Save Another

All the chastening and the hardship is because we are able to bear it. No, we are not able, but we yield to Another—even the Holy Spirit. We are strengthened so that we may endure and so that we may comfort others *"with the comfort with which we ourselves are comforted by God."*

Why do we need brokenness and travail? The reason can be found in the book of Psalms: *"Before I was afflicted I went astray, but now I keep Your word"* (Psalm 119:67). Another passage in Psalms says,

> *Fools, because of their transgression, and because of their iniquities, were afflicted. Their soul abhorred all manner of food, and they drew near to the gates of death. Then they cried out to the LORD in their trouble, and He saved them out of their distresses.* (Psalm 107:17–19)

He saves them? What does the word fool mean? One who knows better than to do what he is doing. *"The fool has said in his heart, 'There is no God'"* (Psalm 53:1), but he knows better. It is only the hardened heart and the stiff neck that are destroyed without remedy. (See Proverbs 29:1.)

YIELDING TO GOD'S PLAN

Now no chastening seems to be joyful for the present, but painful; nevertheless, afterward it yields the peaceable fruit of righteousness to those who have been trained by it. (Hebrews 12:11)

It works out that chastening provokes or bestows upon us fruits unto holiness. It is in the hard places where we see no help that we cry out to God. He delivers us. What for? So that we can help the tempted. It was said of Jesus that He was *"in all points tempted as we are"* (Hebrews 4:15). Where did He receive strength to comfort us? It was at the end of *"strong crying and tears"* (Hebrews 5:7), when the angel came just in time and ministered and saved Him from death. Is He not able? Oh, God highly exalted Him. Now He can send angels to us. When? Just when we are about to go straight down. At such times in the past, did He not stretch out to us a helping hand?

An Interpretation of Tongues:

It is God who sees into the depths of the human heart. He sees and saves those in trouble. There is in it a plan and a purpose for others. How is it worked out? On the line of submission and yielding and a yielding to the unfolding of God's plan. Then we will be able to save others.

[God] *comforts us in all our tribulation, that we may be able to comfort those who are in any trouble, with the comfort with*

which we ourselves are comforted by God.
(2 Corinthians 1:4)

There is a sense of the power of God in humanity bringing you through necessities, never touching the mortal body, only the mind. We must have *"the mind of Christ"* (1 Corinthians 2:16).

CONSOLATION ABOUNDING

"For as the sufferings of Christ abound in us, so our consolation also abounds through Christ" (verse 5). God takes us to a place of need, and before we are barely aware of it, we are full of consolation toward the needy. How? The sufferings of Christ abound! The ministry of the Spirit abounds so often. It is a great blessing. We do not know our calling in the Spirit. It is so much greater than our appreciation of it. Then we speak a word in season (see Isaiah 50:4); here and there we minister, sowing beside all waters as the Holy Spirit directs our paths.

DIVINE COOPERATION

Now if we are afflicted, it is for your consolation and salvation, which is effective for enduring the same sufferings which we also suffer. Or if we are comforted, it is for your consolation and salvation.

(2 Corinthians 1:6)

Paul and the people he ministered to cooperated with one another. Here is the value of testing: it results in a great flow of life from one to another. John Wesley woke up one day and became conscious of the need of one establishing another. In this way, he bore witness to the ministry of the Spirit, and multitudes were born again in his meetings when they heard the wonderful works of God. They heard stories and had consolation poured out to them by the revelation of the Spirit.

We are members of one another. When God's breath is upon us and we are quickened by the Holy Spirit, we can pour into each other wonderful ministries of grace and helpfulness. We need a strong ministry of consolation, not deterioration or living below our privileges.

CONSOLATION RESULTING FROM DEPRIVATION

These consolations come out of deprivation, affliction, and endurance. *"Yes, we had the sentence of death in ourselves, that we should not trust in ourselves but in God who raises the dead"* (2 Corinthians 1:9).

Have we gone as far as Paul? Not one of us has. Can you see how Paul could help and comfort and sustain because he yielded to God all his trust as Jesus did? Because he was yielded to the Holy Spirit to work out the sentence of death, he could help others.

I pray to God that He may never find us *"kick*[ing] *against the goads"* (Acts 9:5). We may have to go through the testing; the truths you stand for, you are tried for. Divine healing, purity of heart, baptism in the Holy Spirit and in fire—we are tested for these truths. We cannot get out of this testing. But in every meeting, the glory rises. We descend down into trials also to be sustained and brought out for the glory of God. *"If God is for us, who can be against us?"* (Romans 8:31). *"For our light affliction, which is but for a moment, is working for us a far more exceeding and eternal weight of glory"* (2 Corinthians 4:17). Oh, the joy of being worthy of suffering! How will I stand the glory that will be after?

> Many of God's people are victorious when suffering but fall away in good times. Deprivation is often easier than success.

There are many of God's people who are victorious in suffering but fail or back out when things are going fine. Deprivation is often easier than success. We need a sound mind all the time to balance us so that we do not trade our liberty for something less.

We get glimpses of the glory all the time. To Paul in the glory, the presence of the Lord was so wonderful. But he said, *"Lest I should be exalted...a thorn in the flesh was given to me"* (2 Corinthians

12:7). That was the mercy of God. *"The Lord knows how to deliver the godly out of temptations"* (2 Peter 2:9) and *"saves such as have a contrite spirit"* (Psalm 34:18). What a revelation for the time to come! If Satan had his way, we would be devoured.

GOD'S GREAT DELIVERANCE

"[God] *delivered us from so great a death, and does deliver us; in whom we trust that He will still deliver us"* (2 Corinthians 1:10).

Hebrews 11:6 tells us that God is! He will never fail us. He has been faithful until this moment, and He will keep us to the end.

> [God] *delivered us from so great a death, and does deliver us; in whom we trust that He will still deliver us, you also helping together in prayer for us, that thanks may be given by many persons on our behalf for the gift granted to us through many.*
> (2 Corinthians 1:10–11)

"[God] *delivered us from so great a death, and does deliver us; in whom we trust that He will still deliver us."* Amen.

nine

Revival—It's Coming, and the Price Is Martyrdom

evival is coming. God's heart is in the place of intense passion. Let us bend or break, for God is determined to bless us. Oh, the joy of service and the joy of suffering! Oh, to be utterly cast upon Jesus! God is coming forth with power. The latter rain is appearing. (See James 5:7.) There must be no coming down from the cross but a going on from faith to faith and from glory to glory, with an increasing diligence so that we may be found in Him without spot and blameless. (See 2 Peter 3:14.)

GOD IS WAITING

A divine plan is working. *"See how the farmer waits for the precious fruit of the earth...until it receives the early and latter rain"* (James 5:7). Jesus is waiting to do all.

Worship is higher than fellowship. Oh, the calmness of meeting with Jesus! All fears are gone. His tender mercy and indescribable peace are ours. I have all if I have Jesus.

God is pruning the tree. The goal of all God's plans for us is a yielded will. God is waiting for the precious fruit of the earth, for the outcome of a sown life, which is to be diviner, lovelier. But first, the seed has to die.

"Great will be the day of Jezreel [which means 'whom God sows' or 'the seed of God']" (Hosea 1:11). *"I will break the bow of Israel in the Valley of Jezreel"* (verse 5).

> *Bow and sword of battle I will shatter from the earth....I will betroth you to Me forever...in righteousness and justice, in lovingkindness and mercy; I will betroth you to Me in faithfulness, and you shall know the LORD....I will answer the heavens, and they shall answer the earth. The earth shall answer with grain, with new wine, and with oil; they shall answer Jezreel* [the seed of God].   (Hosea 2:18–22)

Amen. Let them answer. Let God do it—He commands it. God says, *"'Let there be light!'* (Genesis 1:3). Let your light shine!"

God awaits the death of the seed. How do you know the seed is dead? Why, the green shoots appear. It springs into life. God awaits the evidence of death; He waits for Isaiah 11 to appear—a place of profound rest. Jesus said, *"I will pray the Father, and He will give you another Helper"* (John 14:16).

Let's look at the eleventh chapter of Isaiah together:

There shall come forth a Rod from the stem of Jesse, and a Branch shall grow out of his roots. The Spirit of the LORD shall rest upon Him, the Spirit of wisdom and understanding, the Spirit of counsel and might, the Spirit of knowledge and of the fear of the LORD. His delight is in the fear of the LORD, and He shall not judge by the sight of His eyes, nor decide by the hearing of His ears; but with righteousness He shall judge the poor, and decide with equity for the meek of the earth; He shall strike the earth with the rod of His mouth, and with the breath of His lips He shall slay the wicked. Righteousness shall be the belt of His loins, and faithfulness the belt of His waist. "The wolf also shall dwell with the lamb, the leopard shall lie down with the young goat, the calf and the young lion and the fatling together; and a little child shall lead them. The cow and the bear shall graze; their young ones shall lie down together; and the lion shall eat straw like the ox. The nursing child shall play by the cobra's hole, and the weaned child shall put his hand in the viper's den. They shall not hurt nor destroy in all My holy mountain, for the earth shall be full of the knowledge of the LORD as the waters cover the sea. And in that day there shall be a Root of Jesse, who shall stand as a banner to the people; for the Gentiles shall seek Him, and His resting place shall be glorious." It shall come to pass in that day that the LORD shall set His hand again the second time to recover the remnant of His people who are left, from Assyria and Egypt, from Pathros and Cush, from Elam and Shinar, from Hamath and the islands of the sea. He will set up a banner for the nations, and will assemble the outcasts of Israel, and gather together the dispersed of Judah from the four corners of the earth. Also the envy of Ephraim shall depart, and the adversaries of Judah shall be cut off; Ephraim shall not envy Judah, and Judah shall not harass Ephraim. But they shall fly down upon the shoulder of the Philistines toward the west; together they shall plunder the people of the East; they shall lay their hand on Edom and Moab; and the people of Ammon shall obey them. The LORD will utterly destroy the tongue of the Sea of Egypt; with His mighty wind He will shake His fist over the River, and strike it in the seven streams, and make men cross over dry-shod. There will be a highway for the remnant of His people who will be left from Assyria, as it was for Israel in the day that he came up from the land of Egypt. (Isaiah 11:1–16)

Revival—It's Coming

Not a sound invades the stillness,
    Not a form invades the scene,
Save the voice of my Beloved
    And the person of my King.

Precious, gentle, holy Jesus,
    Blessed Bridegroom of my heart,
In Thy secret inner chamber
    Thou wilt whisper what Thou art.

And within those heavenly places,
    Calmly hushed in sweet repose,
There I drink with joy absorbing
    All the love Thou wouldst disclose.

Wrapt in deep adoring silence,
    Jesus, Lord, I dare not move,
Lest I lose the smallest saying
    Meant to catch the ear of love.

Rest then, oh my soul, contented,
    Thou hast reached that happy place
In the bosom of thy Savior,
    Gazing up in His dear face.

THE EARLY RAIN AND THE LATTER RAIN

The early and the latter rain appear. The early rain is to make the seed die, come to an end, come to ashes. And out of the ashes will come the great fire of consummation, which will burn in the hearts of the people, the Word of the living God producing Christ by the breath of the Spirit.

First ashes, then the latter rain gives a surging of life. The old is finished; now a surging life and the effects of the latter rain will come forth on those who know the Father. A universal outpouring of the Holy Spirit will come. The coming of the Lord is at hand.

The Judge is standing at the door. Has He come? *"When He has come, He will convict the world of sin"* (John 16:8). He has come! *"He will convict the world...of judgment, because the ruler of this world is judged"* (verses 8, 11). Jesus said, *"If I depart, I will send Him [the Helper] to you"* (verse 7). He has come!

> The Holy Spirit wakes up every passion, permits every trial to make the vessel pure.

God waits to move and shake all that can be shaken. Mark 16:17–18 describes the signs following those who believe—an outpouring, mighty and glorious. The early rain gets us ready for that which is to come. Be killed. Be prepared—a vessel ready to pour out torrents.

The baptism of the Holy Spirit is for the death of the seed. The Holy Spirit wakes up every passion, permits every trial. His purpose is to make the vessel pure.

All must die before we see a manifestation of God that is unthought of, undreamed of. It is a call to martyrdom, to death—a call to death! The choice is before you. Decide. Accept the path of death to life. Absolute abandonment is required for a divine equipping. The early and the latter rain appear.

Isaiah 11 is God's equipment for understanding the worldwide purposes of God, the loveliness of Jesus, and the glory of God.

We need revelation for a perishing world. *"Where there is no vision, the people perish"* (Proverbs 29:18 KJV). Wake up! The air is full of revival, but we look for a mighty outpouring that will shake all that can be shaken. Take everything else, but give me vision and revelation of the purposes of God and a wonderful burning love. It is difficult to tell of the freedom of the Holy Spirit in revealing the love of Jesus. *"David spoke to the Lord the words of this song....And he said...my cry entered His ears"* (2 Samuel 22:1–2, 7).

Oh yes, it must come, this surging life—this uttermost death for uttermost life. The early and the latter rain appear. *"We count them blessed who endure"* (James 5:11). *"Beloved, do not think it strange"* (1 Peter 4:12), for the fiery breath of revival is coming. There is a ripple on the lake, a murmur in the air. The price is tremendous: it is martyrdom. We must seal the testimony with our blood. We must die to ourselves. Dying, searching, crucifixions—no resistance. Trust me, it is finished. Yes, be sown first; then comes the revelation of God with eternal issues for multitudes. The latter rain appears. Everything moves before the men whom God has moved, and millions are gathered in, and the heart of God is satisfied.

God says to us,

Since thou art come to that holy room
Where with the choirs of saints forevermore
Thou art made My music,
Tune the instrument here at the door,
And what thou must do then think here before.

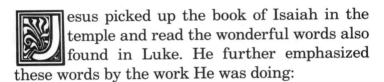

ten

The Spirit of the Lord Is upon Me

Jesus picked up the book of Isaiah in the temple and read the wonderful words also found in Luke. He further emphasized these words by the work He was doing:

> *The Spirit of the LORD is upon Me, because He has anointed Me to preach the gospel to the poor; He has sent Me to heal the brokenhearted, to proclaim liberty to the captives and recovery of sight to the blind, to set at liberty those who are oppressed; to proclaim the acceptable year of the LORD.*
>
> (Luke 4:18–19)

THE IMPORTANCE OF HAVING THE SPIRIT UPON US

I believe God is bringing us to a place where we know the Spirit of the Lord is upon us. If we have not gotten to that place, God wants to bring us to the fact of what Jesus said in John 14: *"I will pray the Father, and He will give you another*

Helper [‘Comforter,’ KJV], that He may abide with you forever” (John 14:16). Because the Spirit of the Lord came upon Him who is our Head, we must see to it that we receive the same anointing, and that the same Spirit is upon us. The Devil will cause us to lose the victory if we allow ourselves to be defeated by him. But it is a fact that the Spirit of the Lord is upon us, and as for me, I have no message apart from the message He will give, and I believe that the signs He speaks of will follow.

I believe that Jesus was the One sent forth from God, and the propitiation for the sins of the whole world. (See 1 John 2:2.) We see the manifestation of the Spirit resting upon Him so that His ministry was with power. May God awaken us to the fact that this is the only place where there is any ministry of power.

In asking the Lord what to say to you, it came to me to arouse you to the fact that the Comforter has come. He has come, and He has come to abide forever. Are you going to be defeated by the Devil? No, for the Comforter has come so that we may receive and give forth the signs that must follow, so that we may not by any means be deceived by the schemes of the Devil. There is no limit to what we may become if we dwell and live in the Spirit. In the Spirit of prayer, we are taken right away from earth into heaven. In the Spirit, the Word of God seems to unfold in a wonderful way, and it is only in the Spirit that the love of God is poured out in us. (See Romans 5:5.)

As we speak in the Spirit, we feel that the fire that burned in the hearts of the two men on their way to Emmaus, when Jesus walked with them, is burning in our hearts. (See Luke 24:13–32.) It is sure to come to pass that when we walk with Him, our hearts will burn; the same power of the Spirit is present to make it happen. The two men on their way to Emmaus could not understand what was happening on the road, but a few hours later, they saw Jesus break the bread, and their eyes were opened.

> There is no limit to what we may become if we dwell and live in the Spirit.

But, beloved, our hearts ought to always burn. There is a place where we can live in the anointing and the clothing of the Spirit, where our words will be clothed with power. *"Do not be drunk with wine...but be filled with the Spirit"* (Ephesians 5:18). Being filled with the Spirit is a wonderful privilege.

I see that it was necessary for John to be in the Spirit on the Isle of Patmos for the revelation to be made clear to him. (See Revelation 1:9–10.) What does it mean to this generation for us to be kept in the Spirit? All human reasoning and all human knowledge cannot be compared with the power of the life that is lived in the Spirit. In the Spirit, we have power to loose and power to bind. (See Matthew 16:19.) There is a place where the Holy Spirit can put us where we cannot be anywhere else but in the Spirit. If we breathe the Holy Spirit's thoughts into our thoughts, and live in the anointing of the Holy Spirit as Jesus lived, then there will be evidences that we are in the Holy Spirit, and we will do His works. But it is only in the Spirit.

Now, I read in Matthew 16:19 that Jesus says, in essence, *"I will give you power to bind, and I will give you power to loose."* This is a power that we have not yet claimed, and we will not be able to claim this manifestation of the Spirit unless we live in the Spirit. When are you able to bind and loose? It is only in the Spirit. You cannot bind things in human strength or with the natural mind. This power was never lacking in Jesus, but I feel as I preach to you tonight that there is a great lack of it in most of us. God help us!

"The Spirit of the LORD is upon Me" (Luke 4:18). Beloved, there was a great purpose in this Spirit being on Jesus, and there is a special purpose in your being baptized in the Spirit. We must not forget that we are members of His body, and by this wonderful baptismal power, we are partakers of His divine nature. (See 2 Peter 1:4.)

The revelation came this way: I saw Adam and Eve driven out of the Garden and a flaming

The Spirit of the Lord Is upon Me

sword at every side to keep them from entering into the Garden. But I saw that all around me was a flaming sword keeping me from evil, and it seemed this would be true if I would claim it, and I said, "Lord, I will." The flaming sword was around me, delivering me from the power of hell. In this way, we are preserved from evil. God is like a wall of fire around us (see Zechariah 2:5); why should we fear? What a wonderful salvation! What a wonderful Deliverer!

Notice Ezekiel 37. The only need of Ezekiel was to be in the Spirit, and while he was in the Spirit, it came to him to prophesy to the dry bones and say, *"O dry bones, hear the word of the Lord"* (verse 4). And as he prophesied according to the Lord's command, he saw an *"exceedingly great army"* (verse 10) rising up about him. The prophet obeyed God's command, and all we have to do is exactly this: obey God. What is impossible with man is possible with God. (See Luke 18:27.)

I pray to God that your spirit, soul, and body may be preserved holy (see 1 Thessalonians 5:23), and that you may be always on fire, always ready with the anointing on you. If this is not so, we are out of divine order, and we ought to cry to Him until the glory comes back upon us.

Spirit-Filled Missionary Work

"The Spirit of the Lord is upon Me" (Luke 4:18). There must have been a reason that the

Holy Spirit was upon Jesus. First of all, it says here,

> *Because He has anointed Me to preach the gospel to the poor; He has sent Me to heal the brokenhearted* [what a Gospel!], *to proclaim liberty to the captives* [what a wonderful Spirit was upon Him!] *and recovery of sight to the blind, to set at liberty those who are oppressed; to proclaim the acceptable year of the LORD.*
>
> (Luke 4:18–19)

You missionaries who are going to India and Africa and China and other places have a wonderful Gospel to take to these people who know nothing about God—a Gospel of salvation and healing and deliverance. If you want to know how missionaries are to work, look at Paul among the natives on the island of Malta. When the viper came out of the fire and fastened onto Paul's hand, they watched to see him swell up and die. When he neither swelled up nor died, they said, "He is a god." (See Acts 28:3–6.)

When you go forth to these dark lands where the Holy Spirit has sent you to preach the unsearchable riches of Christ, to loose the bands of Satan, and to set the captives free, be sure you can say, *"The Spirit of the LORD is upon Me"* (Luke 4:18). Remember that Christ is made unto us not only salvation, but also wisdom and redemption. (See 1 Corinthians 1:30.)

The Spirit of the Lord Is upon Me

"Filled with God, yes, filled with God, pardoned and cleansed and filled with God." Being filled with God leaves no room for doubting or fearing. We have no idea of all that this means—to be filled with God. It means emptied of self. Do you know what it means to be filled with God? It means that you have no fear, for when you are filled with God, you are filled with love, and *"perfect love casts out fear"* (1 John 4:18).

I want to know more about this manifestation of the power of the Holy Spirit. Let us follow Paul further. Next in the twenty-eighth chapter of Acts, we find that the chief of the island had a fever and dysentery. When Paul ministered to him, he was healed, and the people gave Paul things to take with him. (See Acts 28:8–10.)

When we think that the church is poor and needy, we forget that the spirit of intercession can unlock every safe in the world. What did God do for the children of Israel? He took them to vineyards and lands flowing with milk and honey, and all they did was walk in and take possession. If we will only live in the Spirit and the anointing of the Spirit, there will be no lack. There is only lack where faith is not substance, but the Word says faith is the substance (Hebrews 11:1), and whatsoever is not of faith is sin (Romans 14:23). Things will surely come to pass if you will believe this. You do not have to try to bring Christ down; He is down. (See Romans 10:6–8.) You do not have to try to bring Him here; He is here. If we will obey the Lord, there is nothing He will not give us since He has given us Jesus. The Spirit will have to reveal to us the fact that, because the Lord has given us Jesus, He has given us all things.

"The Spirit of the LORD is upon Me" (Luke 4:18). It is true that we must be filled with the Spirit. Father, teach us what this means! It was only because Jesus had an understanding of what it means to be filled with the Spirit that He could stand before those men and say to the demon, "Come out of him." Who is the man who is willing to lay down everything so that he may have God's all? Begin to seek, and don't stop seeking until you know that the Spirit of the Lord is upon you.

"I thank You, Father...that You have hidden these things from the wise and prudent and have revealed them to babes" (Matthew 11:25). If you are in the infant class tonight, the Spirit must have revealed to you your lack. We need to seek with all our hearts. We need to be made flames of fire.

eleven

A Door
of Utterance

*[Pray] also for us, that God would open unto us a
door of utterance, to speak the mystery of Christ,
for which I am also in bonds: that I may make it
manifest, as I ought to speak.*
—Colossians 4:3–4 KJV

aul felt, as we do, the need of utterance.
He had plenty of language, but he wanted
utterance. We can have inspiration, operation, tongue, mind, heart—we need all these. God
works through these in this divine order to give
forth the truth most needed for the time. But the
supreme need of this hour is prayer for utterance.
"*[Pray] also for us, that God would open unto us a
door of utterance...that I may* [speak]*...as I ought.*"

Paul and his helpers were men sent forth by
the power of the Holy Spirit. But without anointing, they could not open the door or give forth the
right word for the hour. Paul and his helpers were
unequal to the need. Was this an indication that
something was out of order? No! For "*unless the*

LORD *guards the city, the watchman stays awake in vain"* (Psalm 127:1). We are dependent on the Holy Spirit to breathe through us. Apart from this living breath of the Spirit, the message is ordinary and not extraordinary.

The question is, How can we live in this place, thrown on omnipotent power? It is by the Spirit of the Lord giving vent, speaking through us. This is not an easy thing. God said to David, "It is good that the desire is in your heart." (See 2 Chronicles 6:8.) But that will not do for us who live in the latter days, when God is pouring forth His Spirit and rivers are at our word. We need to live by Mark 11:22–23: *"Have faith in God....Whoever...believes...will have whatever he says."* In Genesis 1:3, God said, *"Let there be light."* Let God arise. Let God breathe His Spirit through your nature, through your eyes and tongue—the supernatural in the natural for the glory of God. God raised Paul for this ministry,

> We are dependent on the Holy Spirit to breathe His extraordinary message through us.

> *To open their eyes, in order to turn them from darkness to light, and from the power of Satan to God, that they may receive forgiveness of sins and an inheritance among those who are sanctified by faith in Me.* (Acts 26:18)

A Door of Utterance

What was the means? Jesus said, *"By faith in Me."* The faith of God.

The Lord GOD has given Me the tongue of the learned, that I should know how to speak a word in season to him who is weary. He awakens Me morning by morning, He awakens My ear to hear as the learned. The Lord GOD has opened My ear; and I was not rebellious.　　(Isaiah 50:4–5)

Do you believe it? Oh, for more to believe God that *"the tongue of the dumb* [might] *sing"* (Isaiah 35:6). When will they? When they believe and fulfill the conditions. Oh, beloved, it is not easy. But Jesus died and rose again for the possibility. *"Have faith in God"* (Mark 11:22). Be able to say, *"My tongue is the pen of a ready writer"* (Psalm 45:1). The whole man needs to be immersed in God so that the Holy Spirit may operate and the dying world may have the ministry of life for which it is famishing.

But if the Spirit of Him who raised Jesus from the dead dwells in you, He who raised Christ from the dead will also give life to your mortal bodies through His Spirit who dwells in you.　　(Romans 8:11)

As the dead body of Christ was given life and brought out by the Holy Spirit, may we be given eyes to see and ears to hear and a tongue to speak as the oracles of God. *"If anyone speaks, let him speak as the oracles of God"* (1 Peter 4:11). Those are our orders: speaking what no one knows except the Holy Spirit, as the Spirit gives divine utterance—a language that would never come at all unless the Holy Spirit gave utterance and took the things of Christ and revealed them.

I am talking about *"the mystery of Christ."* *"[Pray] also for us, that God would open unto us a door of utterance, to speak the mystery of Christ, for which I am also in bonds: that I may make it manifest, as I ought to speak."* Did God answer these prayers? Yes! *"In mighty signs and wonders, by the power of the Spirit of God...from Jerusalem and round about to Illyricum I have fully preached the gospel of Christ"* (Romans 15:19).

It was the grace of our Lord Jesus Christ, that great Shepherd of the sheep, that brought to us redemption. It was by the grace of God—His favor and mercy, a lavished love and an undeserved favor—that God brought salvation. We did not deserve it.

SEASONED WITH SALT

"Let your speech always be with grace, seasoned with salt" (Colossians 4:6). Salt has three properties: first, it stings; second, it heals; and third, it preserves. In the same way, your words by the Spirit are filled with grace, yet they cut to

the heart, and they bring preservation. We must be very careful to be salty. God's Word will not return void; it will accomplish, and it will prosper (see Isaiah 55:11)—but our mouths must be clean and our desire wholly for God.

Jesus' words were straightforward. To the elite of the holiness movement of His day, He said, *"Woe to you...hypocrites! For you are like white-washed tombs"* (Matthew 23:27). To others He said, "You are deceived; you have the idea that you are the children of Abraham, but you are the children of the Devil, and you do his works." (See John 8:39, 44.) His mouth was full of meekness and gentleness and yet was so salty because of their cor-ruption. Unless you know the charm of Christ, you might think you are out of the working of His eternal power. However, hear what the prophet Isaiah said: *"A bruised reed He will not break"* (Isaiah 42:3). To those for whom there is no lifting up, He comes as the heal-ing Balm of Gilead.

> Here are our orders: speak what no one knows except the Holy Spirit, as the Spirit gives divine utterance.

"Know how you ought to answer each one" (Colossians 4:6). This is not easy to learn. It is only learned in the place of being absorbed by God. When we are in that place, we seek to glorify

God and can give a chastening word full of power to awaken and to save. Use the salt, beloved! Use conviction; use the healing for their preservation.

How true we have to be! You are seasoned with salt. I love it! It is inspiring! It is conviction! Thus the Holy Spirit writes on the fleshly tablets of the temple of the Spirit. (See 2 Corinthians 3:3.) O Lord, enlarge our sense of Your presence in the temple so that we may discern the Lord's body in our midst.

FULL OF THE LIFE OF OUR PRECIOUS LORD

> For He is so precious to me,
>   For He is so precious to me;
> 'Tis heaven below
>   My Redeemer to know,
> For He is so precious to me.

We want our whole being to be so full of the life of our Lord that the Holy Spirit can speak and act through us. We want to live always in Him. Oh, the charm of His divine plan. We cry out for the inspiration of the God of power. We want to act in the Holy Spirit. We want to breathe out life divine. We want the glory, miracles, and wonders that work out the plan of the Most High God. We want to be absorbed by God, and we want to know nothing among men except Jesus and Him crucified (1 Corinthians 2:2). Unto You, O God, be the glory and the honor and the power (Revelation 5:13)!

Yes, filled with God,
   Yes, filled with God,
Emptied of self and filled with God.
Yes, filled with God,
   Yes, filled with God,
Emptied of self and filled with God.

Can you wonder why I love Him so? May there be a cry until we witness Acts 11:15: *"And as I began to speak, the Holy Spirit fell upon them."*

   Oh, be on fire, oh, be on fire,
      Oh, be on fire for God.
   Oh, be on fire, be all on fire,
      Be all on fire for God.

Amen.

twelve

Way, Manifestation, and Ministry

will be referring throughout this message to the third chapter of 2 Corinthians. Three things have been pressing through this morning: first, the way of faith; second, the manifestation of the power of the Spirit; and third, the ministry of the Spirit.

THE MINISTRY OF THE SPIRIT

Now, the ministry of the Spirit has been entrusted to us. The word may be in letter or in power. (See 1 Corinthians 4:20.) We must be in the place of edifying the church. Law is not liberty, but if there is a move of God within you, God has written His laws in your heart so that you may delight in Him. God desires to set forth in us a perfect blending of His life and our life so that we may have abounding inward joy—a place of reigning over all things, not a place of endeavor. Ours is not an endeavor society, but a delight to run in the will of God. There is a great difference between an endeavor and a delight.

Way, Manifestation, and Ministry

God says to us, *"Be holy, for I am holy"* (1 Peter 1:16). Trying will never cause us to reach a place of holiness, but there is a place, or an attitude, where God gives us faith to rest upon His Word, and we delight inwardly over everything. *"I delight to do Your will, O my God"* (Psalm 40:8). There is a place of great joy. Do we want condemnation?

We know there is something within that has been accomplished by the power of God, something greater than there could be in the natural order of the flesh. We are the representatives of Jesus. He was eaten up with zeal. This intense zeal changes us by the operation of the Word; we do not rest in the letter, but we allow the blessed Holy Spirit to lift us by His power.

> Trying will never cause us to reach a place of holiness, but there is a place where God gives us faith to rest upon His Word.

"You are our epistle" (2 Corinthians 3:2). Such a beautiful order prevailed in the Corinthian church; it was a place of holiness and power in Christ, perfect love, and the sweetness of association with Christ.

The disciples were with Jesus three years. He spoke out of the abundance of His heart toward them. John said, "We have touched Him; our eyes have gazed into His eyes." (See 1 John 1:1). Did Jesus know about Judas? Yes. Did He ever tell? No. When Jesus told the disciples that one of them would betray Him, they said, *"Lord, is it I?"* (Matthew 26:22). And Peter said to John, who was close to Jesus, "Find out who it is." The essence of divine order is to bring the church together, so that there is no schism in the body, but a perfect blending of heart to heart.

"The letter kills, but the Spirit gives life" (2 Corinthians 3:6). The sword cut off Malchus's ear, but the Spirit healed it again. (See Luke 22:50–51.) Our ministry has to be in the Spirit, *"free from the law of sin and death"* (Romans 8:2). When we live in the ministry of the Spirit, we are free; in the letter we are bound. If it is *"an eye for an eye"* (Matthew 5:38), we have lost the principle. If we are to come to a place of great liberty, the law must be at an end. Yet we love the law of God; we love to do it and not put one thing aside.

An Interpretation of Tongues:
The way is made into the treasure house of the Most High. As God unfolds the Word, hearts are blended. An incision is being made by the Spirit of the living God, so that we may move, live, act, think, and pray in the Holy Spirit—a new order, life in the Holy Spirit, ministry in the Spirit.

"Clearly you are an epistle of Christ, ministered...by the Spirit of the living God...on tablets of

flesh, that is, of the heart" (2 Corinthians 3:3). It's heart worship when God has made the incision; the Spirit has come to blend with humanity.

BABIES ARE PRECIOUS

There is something beautiful about a baby. Jesus said, *"Whoever humbles himself as this little child is the greatest in the kingdom of heaven"* (Matthew 18:4).

There was a house with ten children and only ten chairs. What was to happen with the baby? When the baby came, every chair was a seat for the baby.

It is a great joy to me to dedicate children, but I believe that when they are old enough, they should be buried in water baptism. (See Romans 6:4.) *"Of such is the kingdom of heaven"* (Matthew 19:14). A baby is a beautiful thing, and God looks on His people at the possibility. The child is lent to us to be brought up in the fear of God.

HAVING GOD'S WORD IN OUR HEARTS

I know He's mine, this Friend so dear;
He lives in me, He's always near.

I want to refer to the word incision. God's Word, our life, is written on the fleshly tablets of the heart.

I was in Rome, where I saw thousands of pilgrims kissing the steps. It made me sorrowful.

How I thank God for His Word! There are many Pentecostal assemblies in Italy, and I saw on the people there a great hunger and thirst after God. God moved mightily among them, and people were saved and baptized in the Holy Spirit in the same meeting.

We must keep in the spiritual tide—God supreme, the altar within the body. Faith is the evidence, the power, and the principle, keeping us in rest. We must have the Spirit in anointing, intercession, revelation, and great power of ministry. To be baptized in the Holy Spirit is to be in God's plan—the Spirit preeminent, revealing the Christ of God, making the Word of God alive—something divine. *"Our sufficiency is from God, who also made us sufficient as ministers of the...Spirit; for the...Spirit gives life"* (2 Corinthians 3:5–6).

I knew a believer whose job was to carry bags of coal. He had been in bed three weeks away from his work. I showed him Romans 7:25: *"I thank God; through Jesus Christ our Lord! So then, with the mind I myself serve the law of God, but with the flesh the law of sin."* I said, "Keep your mind on God and go to work, shouting victory." He did, and the first day he was able to carry a hundred bags, his mind stayed on God and kept in peace.

If your peace is disturbed, there is something wrong. If you are not free in the Spirit, your mind is in the wrong place. Apply the blood of Jesus, and keep your mind stayed upon Jehovah, where "hearts are fully blessed, finding as He promised, perfect peace and rest." Keep your mind on God, gaining strength in Him day by day.

"The law was given through Moses, but grace and truth came through Jesus Christ" (John 1:17). This is a new dispensation, this divine place: Christ in you, the hope and evidence of glory. (See Colossians 1:27.)

An Interpretation of Tongues:
Let your eyes be stayed upon Him, your heart moved by the Spirit, your whole being in a place of refining to come forth as gold. Behold; see the glory. God covers you with a mantle of power.

An Interpretation of Tongues:
For the Lord delights in you, to serve Him with all your heart and strength. Take in all the land, worldwide. Oh, the rest of faith! Ask largely of Him. Until now you have asked nothing.

May God gird you with truth. (See Ephesians 6:14.) I commend you to Him in the name of Jesus. Amen.

thirteen

What Do You Want Me to Do?

As soon as Paul saw the light from heaven that was brighter than the sun, he said, *"Lord, what do You want me to do?"* (Acts 9:6). And as soon as he was willing to yield, he was in a condition where God could meet his need, where God could display His power, where God could have the man.

Beloved, are you saying today, *"What do You want me to do?"* The place of yieldedness is just where God wants us. People are saying, "I want the baptism of the Holy Spirit. I want to be healed. I would like to know for certain that I am a child of God," and I see absolutely nothing, in the way, except that they have not yielded to the plan of God.

In Acts 19:6, the condition was met that Paul demanded, and when he laid his hands on the Ephesian disciples, they were instantly filled with the Spirit and spoke in other tongues and prophesied. The only thing they needed was just to be in the condition where God could come in.

What Do You Want Me to Do?

The main thing today that God wants is obedience. When you begin yielding and yielding to God, He has a plan for your life, and you come in to that wonderful place where all you have to do is eat the fruits of Canaan. I am convinced that Paul must have been in divine order, as well as those men, and Paul had a mission right away to all of Asia.

Brothers and sisters, it is the call of God that counts. Paul was in the call of God. Oh, I believe God wants to stir somebody's heart today to obedience; God may want him to go to China or India or Africa, but the thing God is looking for is obedience. Our words should be, *"Lord, what do You want me to do?"* (Acts 9:6).

Unusual Miracles

Now God worked unusual miracles by the hands of Paul, so that even handkerchiefs or aprons were brought from his body to the sick, and the diseases left them and the evil spirits went out of them.
(Acts 19:11–12)

If God can have His way today, the ministry of somebody will begin. It always begins as soon as a person yields. Paul had been putting many believers in prison, but God brought Paul to such a place of yieldedness and brokenness that he cried out, *"What do You want me to do?"* (Acts 9:6). Paul's choice was to be a bondservant for Jesus Christ.

Beloved, are you willing for God to have His way today? God said about Paul, *"I will show him how many things he must suffer for My name's sake"* (Acts 9:16). But Paul saw that these things were working out *"a far more exceeding and eternal weight of glory"* (2 Corinthians 4:17). You people who have come for a touch from God, are you willing to follow Him? Will you obey Him?

When the Prodigal Son had returned and the father had killed the fatted calf and made a feast for him, the elder brother was angry and said, *"You never gave me a young goat, that I might make merry with my friends"* (Luke 15:29). But the father said to him, *"All that I have is yours"* (verse 31). He could kill a fatted calf at any time. Beloved, everything in the Father's house is ours, but it will come only through obedience. And when He can trust us, we will not come short in anything.

"God worked unusual miracles by the hands of Paul" (Acts 19:11). Let us notice the handkerchiefs that went from his body. This passage indicates that when Paul touched handkerchiefs and sent them forth, God worked special miracles through them, and diseases departed from the sick, and evil spirits went out of them. Isn't this lovely? I believe that after we lay hands on these handkerchiefs and pray over them, they should be handled very sacredly. Even as we carry them, they will bring life, if we carry them in faith to

the suffering ones. The very effect, if you would only believe, would be to change your own body as you carry the handkerchief.

A woman came to me one day and said, "My husband is such a trial to me. The first salary he gets, he spends on drink. Then he cannot do his work and comes home. I love him very much. What can be done?" I said, "If I were you, I would take a handkerchief and would place it under his head when he goes to sleep at night, saying nothing to him but having a living faith." We anointed a handkerchief in the name of Jesus, and she put it under his head. Oh, beloved, there is a way to reach these wayward ones. The next morning on his way to work, he ordered a glass of beer. He lifted it to his lips, but he thought there was something wrong with it, and he put it down and left. He went to another saloon, and another, and did the same thing. He came home sober. His wife was gladly surprised, and he told her the story of how he had been affected. That was the turning point in his life; it meant not only giving up drink, but it meant his salvation.

> God wants us to see that faith is not obtained by struggling and working and longing.

God wants to change our faith today. He wants us to see that it is not obtained by struggling and working and longing. *"The Father Himself loves you"* (John 16:27). *"He Himself took our infirmities and bore our sicknesses"* (Matthew 8:17). *"Come to Me, all you who labor and are heavy laden, and I will give you rest"* (Matthew 11:28). Who is the man who will take the place of Paul and yield and yield and yield until God possesses him in such a way that power will flow from his body to the sick and suffering? It will have to be the power of Christ that flows. Don't think there is some magic power in the handkerchief, or you will miss the power. It is the living faith within the man who lays the handkerchief on his body, and the power of God through that faith. Praise God, we may lay hold of this living faith today. The blood has never lost its power. As we get in touch with Jesus, wonderful things will take place. And what else? We will get nearer and nearer to Him.

THE SECRET OF POWER

There is another side to it:

Then some of the itinerant Jewish exorcists took it upon themselves to call the name of the Lord Jesus over those who had evil spirits, saying, "We exorcise you by the Jesus whom Paul preaches."...And the evil spirit answered and said, "Jesus I know, and Paul I know; but who are you?" (Acts 19:13, 15)

What Do You Want Me to Do?

I implore you in the name of Jesus, especially those of you who are baptized, to wake up to the fact that you have power if God is with you. But there must be a resemblance between you and Jesus. The evil spirit said, "Jesus I know, and Paul I know; but who are you?" Paul had the resemblance. You are not going to get this resemblance without having His presence; His presence changes you. You are not going to be able to get the results without the marks of the Lord Jesus. The man must have the divine power within himself; devils will take no notice of any power if they do not see Christ. "Jesus I know, and Paul I know; but who are you?" The difference in these exorcists was that they did not have the marks of Christ, so the manifestation of the power of Christ was not seen.

If you want power, don't make any mistake about it. If you speak in tongues, don't mistake that for the power. If God has given you revelations along certain lines, don't mistake that for the power. Or if you have even laid hands on the sick and they have been healed, don't mistake that for the power. *"The Spirit of the Lord is upon Me"* (Luke 4:18)—that alone is the power. Don't be deceived. There is a place to be reached where you know the Spirit is upon you so that you will be able to do the works that are accomplished by this blessed Spirit of God in you. Then the manifestation of His power will be seen, and people will believe in the Lord.

What will make men believe the divine promises of God? Beloved, let me say to you today that God wants you to be ministering spirits, and this means being clothed with another power. You know when this divine power is there, and you know when it goes forth. The baptism of Jesus must bring us to the place of having our focus centered on the glory of God; everything else is wasted time and wasted energy. Beloved, we can reach it; it is a high mark, but we can get to it. Do you ask how? Say to God, *"What do You want me to do?"* (Acts 9:6). That is the plan. It means a perfect surrender to the call of God, and perfect obedience.

EXAMPLES OF GOD'S
WONDER-WORKING POWER

A dear young Russian came to England. He did not know the language but learned it quickly and was very much used and blessed by God. As the wonderful manifestations of the power of God were seen, people pressed him to find out the secret of his power, but he felt it was so sacred between him and God that he should not tell it. But they pressed him so much that he finally said to them, "First, God called me, and His presence was so precious that I said to God at every call that I would obey Him. I yielded and yielded and yielded until I realized that I was simply clothed with another power altogether, and I realized that God had taken me—tongue, thoughts, and everything—and I was not myself, but it was Christ working through me."

How many of you today have known that God has called you over and over and has put His hand upon you, but you have not yielded? How many of you have had the breathing of His power within you, calling you to prayer, and you have to confess that you have failed?

I went to a house one afternoon where I had been called, and I met a man at the door. He said, "My wife has not been out of bed for eight months; she is paralyzed. She has been looking forward so much to your coming. She is hoping God will raise her up." I went in and rebuked the Devil's power. She said, "I know I am healed; if you leave, I will get up." I left the house and went away, not hearing anything more about her. I went to a meeting that night, and a man jumped up and said he had something he wanted to say; he had to go to catch a train but wanted to talk first. He said, "I come to this city once a week, and I visit the sick all over the city. There is a woman I have been visiting, and I was very much distressed about her. She was paralyzed and lay on her bed many months. However, when I went there today, she

> God wants you to be ministering spirits, and this means being clothed with another power— His power.

was up doing her work." I tell this story because I want you to see Jesus.

A letter came to our house that said that a young man was very ill. He had been to our mission a few years before with a very bad foot; he had worn no shoe but had fastened a piece of leather around his foot. God had healed him that day. Three years afterward, something else came upon him. What it was I don't know, but his heart failed, and he was helpless. He could not get up or dress or do anything for himself, and in that condition, he called his sister and told her to write to me and see if I would pray. My wife said to go, and she believed that God would give me that life. I went, and when I got to this place, I found that the whole country was expecting me. They had said that when I came, this man would be healed.

I said to the woman when I arrived, "I have come." "Yes," she said, "but it is too late." "Is he alive?" I asked. "Yes, barely alive," she said. I went in and put my hands on him and said, "Martin." He just breathed slightly and whispered, "The doctor said that if I move from this position, I will never move again." I said, "Do you know that the Scripture says, *'God is the strength of my heart and my portion forever'* (Psalm 73:26)"? He said, "Should I get up?" I said, "No."

That day was spent in prayer and ministering the Word. I found a great state of unbelief in that house, but I saw that Martin had faith to be healed. His sister was home from an asylum. God kept me there to pray for that place. I said to the family, "Get Martin's clothes ready; I believe he is to be raised up." I felt the unbelief.

I went to the chapel and had prayer with a number of people around there, and before noon they, too, believed that Martin would be healed. When I returned, I said, "Are his clothes ready?" They said, "No." I said, "Oh, will you hinder God's work in this house?"

I went into Martin's room all alone. I said, "I believe God will do a new thing today. I believe that when I lay hands on you, the glory of heaven will fill this place." I laid my hands on him in the name of the Father, Son,

> The Holy Spirit wants you for the purpose of manifesting Jesus through you.

and Holy Spirit, and immediately the glory of the Lord filled the room, and I fell at once to the floor. I did not see what took place on the bed or in the room, but this young man began to shout out, "Glory, glory!" and I heard him say, "For Your glory, Lord," and he stood before me perfectly healed. He went to the door and opened it, and his father stood there. He said, "Father, the Lord has raised me up," and the father fell to the floor and cried for salvation. The young woman brought out of the asylum was perfectly healed at that moment by the power of God in that house.

God wants us to see that the power of God coming upon people has something more in it than we have yet known. The power to heal and to baptize is in this place, but you must say, *"Lord, what do You want me to do?"* (Acts 9:6). You say it is four months before the harvest. If you had the eyes of Jesus, you would see that the harvest is already here. (See John 4:35.) The Devil will say you can't have faith. Tell him he is a liar. The Holy Spirit wants you for the purpose of manifesting Jesus through you. Oh, may you never be the same again! The Holy Spirit moving upon us will make us to be like Him, and we will truly say, *"Lord, what do You want me to do?"*

fourteen

Workers Together with God

An Interpretation of Tongues:
God has come to visit us, and He has revealed Himself unto us, but He wants you to be so ready that nothing that He says will miss. He wants to build you on the foundation truth.

Are you ready? "Why?" you ask. Because God has something even better than what He gave us yesterday. He wants to give us higher ground, holier thoughts, and a more concentrated, clearer ministry. God wants us to be in a rising tide every day. This rising tide is a changing of faith; it is an attitude of the spirit; it is where God rises higher and higher.

God wants us to come to the place where we will never look back. God has no room for the person who looks back, thinks back, or acts back.

The Holy Spirit wants to get you ready to stretch yourself out to God and to believe that

"He is a rewarder of those who diligently seek Him" (Hebrews 11:6). You do not need to use vain repetitions when you pray. (See Matthew 6:7.) Simply ask and believe. Do more believing and less begging.

People come with their needs, they ask, and then they leave with their needs because they do not faithfully wait to receive what God has promised them. If they ask for it, they will get it.

Many people are missing the highest order. I went to a person who was full of the Spirit but was constantly saying, "Glory! Glory! Glory!" I said, "You are full of the Holy Spirit, but the Spirit cannot speak because you continually speak." He kept still then, and the Spirit began to speak through him. This story illustrates the fact that often we are altogether in God's way.

I want to so change your operation in God that you will know that God is operating through you for this time and forevermore. May the Spirit awaken us to deep things today.

Are you ready? "What for?" you ask. To move and be moved by the mighty power of God that cannot be moved, and to be so chastened and built up that you are in the place where it doesn't matter where the wind blows or what difficulty comes because you are fixed in God.

Are you ready? "What for?" you ask. To come into the plan of the Most High God, believing what the Scriptures say and holding fast to what is good, believing so that no one will take your crown. (See Revelation 3:11.)

THE WORD CHANGES THE BELIEVER

God can so change us by His Word day by day that we are altogether different. David knew this. He said, *"Your word has given me life"* (Psalm 119:50). *"He sent His word and healed them"* (Psalm 107:20). How beautiful that God can make His Word abound! *"Your word I have hidden in my heart, that I might not sin against You!"* (Psalm 119:11).

It is absolute disloyalty and unbelief to pray about anything in the Word of God. The Word of God does not need to be prayed about: the Word of God needs to be received. If you will receive the Word of God, you will always be in a big place. If you pray about the Word of God, the Devil will be behind the whole thing. Never pray about anything concerning which it can be said, "Thus says the Lord." You need to receive God's words so that they will build you on a new foundation of truth.

Let us look at a very important verse in the book of Romans:

I beseech you therefore, brethren, by the mercies of God, that you present your bodies a living sacrifice, holy, acceptable to God, which is your reasonable service.

(Romans 12:1)

We see in this verse that the writer, Paul, had been operated on. He had undergone a mighty operation on more than just a surgical table. He had been cut to the very depths of his being, until he had absolutely reached a place on the altar of full surrender. When he came to this place, out of the depths of this experience, he gave his whole life, as it were, in a nutshell.

> You need to receive God's words so that they will build you on a new foundation of truth.

Now, I want to turn your attention to the sixth chapter of 2 Corinthians, which was also written by Paul. This is a summit position for us, although there are many lines to be examined to see if we are rising to the summit of these glorious experiences. This passage is also the groundwork of deep heart searching. It is divine revelation of the spiritual character to us. Paul must have been immersed in this holy place.

Here we have again a beautiful word that ought to bring us to a very great place of hearing by the hearing of faith: *"We then, as workers together with Him"* (2 Corinthians 6:1).

This verse is a collective thought; it preaches to the whole church in Christ Jesus. Paul had the Corinthians in mind because the Corinthian church was the first church among the Gentiles, and he was the Apostle to the Gentiles.

Do Not Receive God's Grace in Vain

"We then, as workers together with Him also plead with you not to receive the grace of God in vain" (verse 1). This is one of the mightiest verses in the Scriptures. People are getting blessed all the time and are receiving revelation all the time, and they go from one point to another, but they do not establish themselves in the thing that God has brought to them.

If you do not let your heart be examined when the Lord comes with blessing or with correction, if you do not make the blessing or the correction a stepping-stone, or if you do not make it a rising place, then you are receiving the grace of God in vain. People could be built up much more in the Lord and be more wonderfully established if they would step out sometimes and think over the graces of the Lord.

Grace will be multiplied on certain conditions. How? In the first chapter of 2 Timothy, we have these words: *"The genuine faith that is in you"* (verse 5). Everyone in the entire church of God has the same precious faith within him. If you allow this same precious faith to be foremost, utmost in everything, you will find that grace and peace are multiplied.

Just the same, the Lord comes to us with His mercy, and if we do not see that the God of grace and mercy is opening to us the door of mercy and utterances, we are receiving His grace in vain.

I thank God for every meeting. I thank God for every blessing. I thank God every time a person says to me, "God bless you, brother!" I say, "Thank you, brother. The Lord bless you!" We are in a very great place when people desire for us to be blessed.

If we want strength in building our spiritual character, we should never forget our blessings. When you are in prayer, remember how near you are to the Lord and how dear that is. Prayer is a time during which God wants you to be strengthened, and He wants you to remember that He is with you.

When you open the sacred pages and the light comes right through and you say, "Oh, isn't that wonderful!" thank God, for it is the grace of God that has opened your understanding. When you go to a church meeting and the revelation comes forth and you feel that it is what you needed, receive it as the grace of God. He has brought you to a place where He might make you a greater blessing.

CONSTANT SALVATION

For He says: "In an acceptable time I have heard you, and in the day of salvation I have helped you." Behold, now is the accepted time; behold, now is the day of salvation. (2 Corinthians 6:2)

There are two processes of salvation. First, God helped you when the Spirit was moving you and when the Adversary was against you, when your neighbors and friends did not want you to be saved, and when everybody rose up in accusation against you. When you knew there was fighting on the outside and fighting within, He helped you; He covered you until you came into salvation. And then, second, He keeps you in the plan of His salvation.

This is the day of salvation. The fact that you are being saved does not mean that you were not saved, but it means that you are being continually changed. In the process of regeneration, you are being made like God; you are being brought into the operation of the Spirit's power; you are being made like Him.

> The fact that you are being saved does not mean that you were not saved; instead it means you are being continually changed.

This is the day of salvation. He has helped you in a time when Satan would destroy you, and He is with you now.

This is the day of salvation. If we remain stationary, God has nothing for us. We must see that we must progress. Yesterday will not do for today. I must thank God for yesterday. However, tomorrow is affected by what I am today.

Today is a day of inspiration and divine intuition, a day in which God is enrapturing the heart, breaking all shorelines, getting my heart to the place where it is responsive only to His cry, where I live and move honoring and glorifying God in the Spirit. This is the day of the visitation of the Lord. This is the great day of salvation, a day of moving on for God.

An Interpretation of Tongues:
It is the Lord. Let Him do what seems good to Him. It may be death, but He has life in the midst of death.

We will praise and magnify the Lord, for He is worthy to be praised! He has helped us, and now He is building us; now He is changing us; now we are in the operation of the Holy Spirit. Every day you must climb to higher ground. You must deny yourself in order to go forward with God. You must refuse everything that is not pure and holy and separate. God wants you to be pure in heart. He wants your intense desire after holiness.

"Seek first the kingdom of God and His righteousness, and all these things shall be added to you" (Matthew 6:33).

IN PERFECT HARMONY

"Give no offense in anything, that our ministry may not be blamed" (2 Corinthians 6:3). That is lovely. Oh, the church can be built! God will break down opposing things.

If you, being a member of a certain church, are in a place where you would rather see one person saved at your church than two people saved at another church, then you are altogether wrong, and you need to be saved. You are still out of the order of the Spirit of God, and you are a stranger to true, holy life with God.

If your ministry is not to be blamed, how can you help to prevent it from being blamed? You have to live in love. See to it that you never say or do anything that would interfere with the work of the Lord; rather, live in the place where you are helping everybody, lifting everybody, and causing everybody to come into perfect harmony. Remember, there is always a blessing where there is harmony. *"One accord"* is the keynote of the victory that is going to come to us all the time.

There are thousands and thousands of different churches, but they are all one in the Spirit to the extent that they receive the life of Christ. If there is any division, it is always outside of the Spirit. The spiritual life in the believer never has known dissension, because where the Spirit has perfect liberty, there is total agreement, and there is no schism in the body.

"The letter kills, but the Spirit gives life" (2 Corinthians 3:6). When there is division, it is only because people choose the letter instead of the Spirit. If we are in the Spirit, we will have life. If we are in the Spirit, we will love everybody. If we are in the Spirit, there will be no division; there will be perfect harmony.

God wants to show us that we must so live in the Spirit that the ministry is not blamed.

It is a wonderful ministry God has given to us because it is a life ministry. Pentecostal positions are spiritual positions. We recognize the Holy Spirit, but we recognize first the Spirit giving us life, saving us from every form of evil power, transforming our human nature until it is in divine order. Then, in that divine order, we see that the Lord of Hosts can very beautifully arrange the life until we live in the Spirit and are not fulfilling the lusts of the flesh. (See Galatians 5:16.) I like that because I see that when the Holy Spirit is perfectly in charge, He lifts and lightens and unveils the truth in a new way until we grasp it.

An Interpretation of Tongues:
Do not let your good be spoken of as evil, but so live in the spiritual life with Christ that He is being glorified over your body, your soul, and your spirit, until your very life becomes emblematic and God reigns over you in love and peace.

Oh, how wonderful it would be if every one of us would possess this word in our hearts: *"Do not let your good be spoken of as evil"* (Romans 14:16). I know we all want to be good. It is not a wrong thing to desire that our goodness be appreciated. But we must watch ourselves because it is an evil day (although it is the day of salvation), and we must understand these days that the Lord wants to chasten and bring a people right into a full-tide position.

I believe that it is just as possible for God to sweep a group of believers right into glory before the Rapture as during the Rapture. It is possible for you to be taken even if others are left. May God give us a very keen inward discerning of our hearts' purity. We want to go to heaven—it is far better for us to go—but it is far better for the church that we stay. (See Philippians 1:23–24.)

Paul realized the following truth: *"To depart* [to] *be with Christ...is far better"* (verse 23). Then there is another side to it. Believing that God made us for the proclamation of the Gospel, for the building of the church, we would say, "Lord, for the purpose of being a further blessing for Your sake and for the sake of the church, just keep us full of life to stay." We do not want to be full of disease, but we want to be full of life.

May the Lord grant to us right now a living faith to believe.

In Affliction for the Church

"But in all things we commend ourselves as ministers of God: in much patience, in tribulations, in needs, in distresses" (2 Corinthians 6:4). Now, these tribulations are not the tribulations of various diseases. Paul is very definite along

these lines. He suffered tribulations with the people. Jesus suffered tribulations with the people. There can be many tribulations within our human frame along the lines of feeling that our spiritual influence is not bearing fruit in the lives of others.

You have to so live in the Spirit that when you see the church not rising into its glory, you suffer tribulation for the church. You are very sorry and deeply distressed because the church is not capturing the vision, and there is tribulation in your sorrow.

> This is the way of God's church: the church rising to a higher height, a glorious truth, a blessed faithfulness.

God wants us to be so spiritual that we have perfect discernment of the spirit of the people. However, if I can in a moment discern the spirit in a meeting, whether it is life-giving, whether the whole church is receiving it, whether my heart is moved by this power, then I can also see faith waning, and that will bring tribulation and trouble to my life.

May God give us the realization that we are so joined to the church that we may labor to bring the church up. Paul said that he labored in birth in order that Christ might be formed in the people again. (See Galatians 4:19.) He was not laboring so that they could be saved again. No, but they had lacked perception; they had missed fellowship of the divine order; so he labored again so that they might be brought into this deep fellowship in the Spirit.

May God help us to see that we can labor for the church. Blessed is the person who can weep between the church door and the altar. Blessed are the people of God who can take someone else's church on their hearts and weep and cry through until the church is formed again, until she rises in glory, until the power of heaven is over her, until the spiritual acquaintance rises higher and higher, until a song lifts her to the heights.

This is the order of the church of God: the ministry not being blamed, but the church rising to a higher height, a glorious truth, a blessed faithfulness, higher and higher.

Possess Your Soul in Peace

"In much patience" (2 Corinthians 6:4). That is an important message for these days. I know I am speaking to people who have churches and who have a lot of responsibilities in churches. Remember this: you never lose as much as when you lose your peace. If the people see that you have lost your groundwork of peace, they know that you have gotten outside of the position of victory. You have to possess your soul in peace.

Strange things will happen in the church. All circumstances will appear to be against the church, and you will feel that the Enemy is busy. At that time, possess your soul in peace. Let the people know that you are acquainted with One *"who, when He was reviled, did not revile in return"* (1 Peter 2:23).

Possess patience to such an extent that you can suffer anything for the church, for your friends, for your neighbors, or for anyone. Remember this: we build character in others as our character is built. As we are pure in our thoughts, are tender and gracious to other people, and possess our souls in patience (see Luke 21:19), then people have a great desire for our fellowship in the Holy Spirit.

Now, Jesus is an example to us along these lines. The people saw Him undisturbed. I love to think about Him. He helps me so much because He is the very essence of help.

Do Not Give Offense or Cause Distress

"In needs, in distresses" (2 Corinthians 6:4). This verse is referring to spiritual distresses that are a result of acquaintance with the church. It is the church we are dealing with here. Paul was in a place where he was speaking by divine appointment to the church.

The purpose of these meetings is to gather the church together along the lines of faithfulness, because if ten people could have saved Sodom and Gomorrah, ten holy people in a church can hold the power of the Spirit until light reigns. We do not want to seek to save ourselves; on the contrary, we want to lose ourselves so that we may save the church. (See Matthew 16:25.) You cannot stop distresses from coming; they will come, and offenses will come. But woe to those who cause offenses. (See Matthew 18:7.) See that you do not cause offense. See that you live on a higher plane. See that your tongue does not speak evil of others.

I wonder if you have ever fully seen the picture presented in the twenty-sixth chapter of Matthew. Jesus said, *"One of you will betray Me"* (verse 21). The disciples asked, *"Lord, is it I?"* (verse 22). Every one of them was so conscious of his human weaknesses that not a single one of them could say that it would not be he.

> Remember this: we build character in others as our character is built.

John was leaning on the Lord, and Peter motioned to him and said, "Please find out who it is." He knew that if anybody could find out, it would be John.

How long do you think Jesus had known? He had known for at least close to three years. Jesus had been with them, He had been feeding them, He had been walking up and down with them, and He had never told any of them it was Judas.

Those who follow Jesus should be so sober and sensitive that they would not speak against someone else, whether the words were true or not.

Jesus is the great Personality. In every way, I need to listen to Him and also be motivated by His holy inward generosity, His purity, and His acquaintance with love.

If Jesus had told the disciples that Judas would one day betray Him, what would have been the result? Everyone would have been bitter against Judas. So He saved all His disciples from being bitter against Judas for three years.

What love! Can't you see that holy divine Savior? If we saw Him clearly, every one of us would throw ourselves at His feet. If we had a crown worth millions of dollars, we would cast it at His feet and say, "You alone are worthy, Lord." O God, give us such a holy, intense, divine acquaintance with You that we would rather die than grieve You! Oh, for inward character that will make us say, "A thousand deaths rather than sinning once." O Jesus, we worship You! You alone are worthy!

An Interpretation of Tongues:

Into the very depths have I gone to help you. And in the very depths I called you my own, and I delivered you when you were oppressed and in oppression, and I brought you out when you were sure to sink below the waves, and I lifted you and brought you into the banqueting house.

It is the mercy of the Lord. It is the love of the Lord. It is the grace of the Lord. It is the Spirit of the Lord. It is the will of the Lord.

Be ready and alert for God. Live in the Holy Spirit. Oh, I understand the Scripture that says,

> *I wish you all spoke with tongues, but even more that you prophesied; for he who prophesies is greater than he who speaks with tongues, unless indeed he interprets, that the church may receive edification.*
> (1 Corinthians 14:5)

I pray to God that we may learn the lesson of how to keep ourselves so that the Spirit will blend us, making the harmony beautiful. There is not a person in this place who is not feeling the breath of the Almighty over us. This is one of those moments when the Spirit is coming to us and saying, "Don't forget, this is the receiving of the grace of God." You are not to go away and forget; you are to go away and be what God intends for you to be.

ARRESTED IN SWEDEN

"In stripes, in imprisonments, in tumults, in labors, in sleeplessness, in fastings" (2 Corinthians 6:5). How those first apostles did suffer! And how we do suffer together with them.

Sweden is a most remarkable place in many ways. When I was in Sweden, the power of God was upon me, and it was there that I was arrested for preaching these wonderful truths, for talking about the deep things of God, and for being used by God to heal all kinds of people.

A certain denomination, along with a group of doctors, rose up like an army against me and had special meetings with the king to try to get me thrown out of the country. At last they succeeded. It was in Sweden that I was escorted out by two detectives and two policemen because of the mighty power of God moving among the people in Stockholm. But, beloved, it was very lovely!

> Faith is the great operating position. When we believe God, all things are easy.

One of the nurses in the king's household came to a meeting, and she was healed of leg trouble—I forget whether it was a broken thighbone or a dislocated joint. She went to the king and said, "I have been so wonderfully healed by this man. You know I am walking all right now."

"Yes," he said, "I know everything about him. Tell him to go. I do not want him to be turned out. If he leaves, he can come back; but if he is turned out, he cannot come back."

I thank God I was not turned out—I was escorted out.

Some of the people went to see the police to see if I could have a big meeting in the park on the following Monday. The policemen joined together and said, "There is only one reason that we could refuse him, and it is this: if that man puts his hands on the sick in the great park, it would take thirty more policemen to guard the situation. But if he will promise us that he will not lay his hands on the people, then we will allow him to use the park."

The people came and asked me if I would agree to the police's stipulation, and I said, "Promise them. I know God is not subject to my laying hands on the people. When the presence of the Lord is there to heal, it does not require hands. Faith is the great operation position. When we believe God, all things are easy."

So they built a platform where I could speak to thousands of people.

I prayed, "Lord, You know. You have never yet been powerless in any place. You know all things; show me how these people can be healed today without having hands laid on them. Show me."

To the people I said, "All of you who would like the power of God to go through you today, healing everything, put your hands up."

There was a great crowd of hands; thousands of hands went up.

"Lord, show me."

And He told me as clearly as anything to pick a person out who stood on a rock. So I told them all to put their hands down except that person. To her I said, "Tell all the people your troubles."

She began to relate her troubles. From her head to her feet she was in so much pain that she felt that if she did not sit down or lie down she would never be able to go on.

"Lift your hands high," I said. Then, "In the name of Jesus, I rebuke from your head to your feet the Evil One, and I believe that God has loosed you."

Oh, how she danced and how she jumped and how she shouted!

That was the first time that God revealed to me that He could heal without the laying on of hands. We had hundreds healed without touching them and hundreds saved without touching them. Our God is a God of mighty power.

Oh, how wonderful, how glorious, and how fascinating it is that we can come into a royal place! This is a royal place: we have a great God; we have a wonderful Jesus. I believe in the Holy Spirit.

IN PRISON IN SWITZERLAND

"In imprisonments" (2 Corinthians 6:5). In Switzerland, I have been put into prison twice for this wonderful work. But, praise God, I was brought out all right!

The officers said to me, "We find no fault. We are so pleased. We have found no fault because you are such a great blessing to us in Switzerland." And in the middle of the night, they said, "You can go."

I said, "No. I will only go on one condition—that is, that every officer in the place gets down on his knees and I pray with all of you."

Glory to God!

A HIGH TIDE

Are you ready? "What for?" you ask. To believe the Scriptures. That is necessary. The Scriptures are the foundation that we must have in order to build properly. Christ is the cornerstone; we are all in the building.

Oh, if I could let you see that wonderful city coming down out of heaven! It is made up of millions, trillions, countless numbers of people. It is a city of people coming down out of heaven to be married. (See Revelation 21:2.)

Get ready for that. Claim your rights in God's order. Do not give way. Have faith in God. Believe the Scriptures are for you. If you want a high tide that is rising in the power of God, say, "Lord, give me what I need so that I will be lacking in nothing." Have a real faith. Believe that love covers you, that His life flows through you, that His life-giving Spirit lifts you. This is my prayer:

O God, take these people into Your great pavilion. Lead them, direct them, preserve them, strengthen them, uphold them by Your mighty power. Let the peace that passes understanding, the joy of the Lord, the comfort of the Holy Spirit, be with them. Amen.

fifteen

Questions Answered

Q: What should be our attitude toward the coming of the Lord? Should we be enjoying His personal presence now, disregarding the time of His coming, or should we wait for and anticipate His coming?

A: Do what Peter did: he hastened toward Christ's coming (see 2 Peter 3:12), and he left everything behind him to catch a glimpse of it. You have to keep your mind on it, looking toward and hastening it. Christ's coming is a joy to the church; it is that *"blessed hope"*; it is that *"glorious appearing"* (Titus 2:13). Keeping your mind on it will save you from a number of troubles, for he who looks for it purifies himself. (See 1 John 3:2–3.)

Q: Does the wrestling referred to in the following passage mean wrestling in prayer?

> *For we do not wrestle against flesh and blood, but against principalities, against powers, against the rulers of the darkness of this age, against spiritual hosts of wickedness in the heavenly places.*
>
> (Ephesians 6:12)

A: According to 2 Corinthians, we are able to strike the Enemy and bring every thought into perfect obedience to the law of Christ:

> *Casting down arguments ["imaginations," KJV] and every high thing that exalts itself against the knowledge of God, bringing every thought into captivity to the obedience of Christ.*
>
> (2 Corinthians 10:5)

Now, are we able to do this through prayer or through something else? It is quite clear to me that faith inspires us to pray, but faith will command us to command. If we are in the place of real faith, when opposition comes against us, we will say, *"Get behind me"* (Matthew 16:23), no matter what it is.

Prayer is without accomplishment unless it is accompanied by faith. Jude said we can pray in the Holy Spirit. (See Jude 20.) Be sure that you are filled with the Spirit, that it is not you who is praying but Another. Be sure that you are filled with the life of Christ until faith rises, claims, destroys, and brings down imaginations and everything that opposes Christ.

Q: Which is the right way to baptize—in the name of Jesus, or in the name of the Father, Son, and Holy Spirit?

A: Water baptism in the name of Jesus causes more trouble than anything else, and we should never have trouble in the church; we should be at peace. The Lord said that we are to baptize in the name of the Father, Son, and Holy Spirit (see Matthew 28:19), and when we stay in the right order, as He said, then there is no schism in the body.

When we do things our own way and set out on a new path, we cause dissension and trouble. Baptizing in the name of Jesus has caused more trouble than anything else because people have not been satisfied to stop there; they have gone further and said that Jesus is the Father, Jesus is the Son, and Jesus is the Holy Spirit. If we do not keep on the right track, adhering to the words that Jesus spoke, we will be toppled over in awful distress and darkness. Stay on the high road.

Q: Does a person have to go to school in order to save souls?

A: I think a believer will save more souls outside of school. What we have to understand is that soul-saving work is never made in schools. Soul-saving work is the regeneration of the spirit, of the life; it causes a believer to be eaten up with the zeal of the Lord. Soul saving is the best thing; it is the sure place, the right place, and I hope we are doing it when Christ comes.

Q: What is meant when it is said that Jesus *"did not consider it robbery to be equal with God"* (Philippians 2:6)?

A: It means that Jesus was equal with God in power, in authority, and in glory. He was perfectly one with the Father. (See John 10:30.) What His Father was, He was; they were perfectly joined. Yet in order to act in perfect obedience, so that all people could learn obedience, He left heaven, left everything behind, to save us. He had the right to stop and say, "Father, You go," but He was willing to go. He left heaven even though He had the right not to leave.

Q: Suppose that a contract is entered into by two people and is then broken by one party. Should damages be collected by law by the other party?

A: Yes, if you live in the law. But if you live in the Spirit, then you will not go to law with your brother. So, the answer depends on whether you live in law or live in grace. If you live in grace, you will never go into law.

I thank God that although I was in business for twenty-five years and might have picked up a lot of money, it is still there because I would not go to law. I do not believe in it.

But I am not a law to you people. I tell you what law is and what grace is.

Q: What is the seal put upon God's people?

A: The seal is the Holy Spirit. It is different from anything else. It is upon you, and the Devil knows it; all the evil powers of the earth know it. You are sealed with the Holy Spirit of promise until the day of redemption. (See Ephesians 1:13–14.) You are also baptized in the same Spirit, and that truth is in the Epistles.

All who are in Christ will be *"caught up"* (1 Thessalonians 4:17) at His coming. The twenty-second chapter of Luke distinctly says that Jesus will not sit down again to break bread until the kingdom has come (verses 15–16). Now, the kingdom is in every believer, and Jesus will not sit down until every believer is there. The kingdom is in the believer, and the kingdom will come, and I am sure millions and millions of people will be there who were never baptized with the Holy Spirit but had the life of Christ inside. It is not the Holy Spirit who is the life: Christ is the life. (See Colossians 3:4.) When Christ comes, who is our life, we will go to Him.

Q: Is it every Christian's privilege to have his eyes so preserved that he never needs to wear glasses?

A: The aging process affects every person. There are many people who have been praying ever since they were ten years old, and if praying and the life within them could have altered the situation, it would have been altered. But I see that many are here today with gray hair and white hair; this shows that the natural man decays, and you cannot do what you like with it. But the supernatural man may so abound in the natural man that it never decays; it can be replaced by divine life.

There comes a time in life when at age fifty or so, all eyes, without exception, begin to grow dim. However, although the natural man has had a change, I believe and affirm that the supernatural power can be so ministered to us that even our eyesight can be preserved right through. But I say this: any person who professes to have faith and then gets a large print Bible so that he will not need glasses is a fool. It presents a false impression before the people. He must see that if he wants to carry a Bible that is not huge, his eyesight may require some help, or he may not be able to read correctly.

> I believe that His supernatural power can be so ministered to us that even our eyesight can be preserved.

I have been preaching faith to my people for thirty years. When my daughter came back from Africa and saw her mother and me with glasses, she was amazed. When our people saw us put glasses on the first time, they were very troubled. They were no more troubled than we were. But I found it was far better to be honest with the people and acknowledge my condition than get a Bible with large print and deceive the people and say that my eyesight was all right. I like to be honest.

Questions Answered

My eyesight gave way at about age fifty-three, and somehow God is doing something. I am now sixty-eight, and I do not need a stronger prescription than I needed then, and I am satisfied that God is restoring me.

When I was seeking this way of divine healing, I was baffled because all the people who had mighty testimonies of divine healing were wearing glasses. I said, "I cannot go on with this thing. I am baffled every time I see the people preaching divine healing wearing glasses." And I got such a bitterness in my spirit that God had to settle me along that line—and I believe that I have not yet fully paid the price.

My eyes will be restored, but until then, I will not deceive anybody. I will wear glasses until I can see perfectly.

A woman came up to me one day, and I noticed that she had no teeth. "Why," I said, "your mouth is very uneven. Your gums have dropped in some places, and they are very uneven."

"Yes," she said, "I am trusting the Lord for a new set of teeth."

"That is very good," I said. "How long have you been trusting Him for them?"

"Three years."

"Look here," I said, "I would be like Gideon. I would put the fleece out, and I would tell the Lord that I would trust Him to send me teeth in ten days or money to buy a set in ten days. Whichever came first, I would believe it was from Him."

In eight days, fifty dollars came to her from a person whom she had never been acquainted with in any way, and it bought her a beautiful set of teeth—and she looked nice in them.

Often I pray for a person's eyesight, and as soon as he is prayed for, he believes, and God stimulates his faith, but his eyesight is about the same. "What should I do?" he asks. "Should I go away without my glasses?"

"Can you see perfectly?" I ask. "Do you need any help?"

"Yes. If I were to go without my glasses, I would stumble."

"Put your glasses on," I say, "for when your faith is perfected, you will no longer need your glasses. When God perfects your faith, your glasses will drop off. But as long as you need them, use them."

You can take that for what you like, but I believe in common sense.

sixteen

Our Calling:

Part One

Beloved, I believe that the Lord would have us this morning to consider the gifts. I will more or less be speaking to preachers and to those who desire to be preachers. I want to speak to you from the fourth chapter of Ephesians. We will begin with the first verse:

I, therefore, the prisoner of the Lord, beseech you to walk worthy of the calling with which you were called, with all lowliness and gentleness, with longsuffering, bearing with one another in love, endeavoring to keep the unity of the Spirit in the bond of peace. There is one body and one Spirit, just as you were called in one hope of your calling; one Lord, one faith, one baptism; one God and Father of all, who is above all, and through all, and in you all. But to each one of us grace was given according to the measure of Christ's gift. Therefore He says: "When He ascended on high, He led

*captivity captive, and gave gifts to men."
(Now this, "He ascended"; what does it
mean but that He also first descended into
the lower parts of the earth? He who descended is also the One who ascended far
above all the heavens, that He might fill
all things.) And He Himself gave some to
be apostles, some prophets, some evangelists, and some pastors and teachers, for
the equipping of the saints for the work
of ministry, for the edifying of the body of
Christ, till we all come to the unity of the
faith and of the knowledge of the Son of
God, to a perfect man, to the measure of
the stature of the fullness of Christ.*

(Ephesians 4:1–13)

CALLED BY GOD TO PREACH THE GOSPEL

I would like to utter those same words that
Paul uttered in 1 Corinthians 14:5: *"I wish you all
spoke with tongues, but even more that you prophesied."* I believe that there is no way to make
proclamation but by the Spirit. And I believe that
those who are sent are chosen and called by God
to be sent. And so, as we study this passage from
Ephesians, I trust that everyone will understand
what his calling is in the Spirit, and what the Lord
demands of us as preachers.

In the face of God and in the presence of His
people, we should be able to behave ourselves in

a way that is so appropriate and pleasing to the Lord that we always leave behind us a life of blessing and power without creating strife.

It is a great choice to become a preacher of the Gospel, to handle the Word of Life. We who handle the Word of Life ought to be well equipped in the areas of common sense and judgment, and we must not be given to anything that is contrary to the Word of God. There should always be in us such deep reverence toward God and His Word that under all circumstances we would not forfeit our principles along the lines of the faith that God has revealed to us by the truth.

> The Word of God gives strength to weakness in all who hear it and brings oil to the troubled heart.

Today I believe God will show us how wonderful we may be in the order of the Spirit, for God wants us to be always in the Spirit. He wants us to rightly divide the Word of Truth (see 2 Timothy 2:15) so that it will give strength to weakness in all who hear it. It will bring oil to the troubled heart. It will bring rest. The Word of God will make us know that, having done all, we may stand in the trial. (See Ephesians 6:13.)

God wants us to know that there is strength by the power of the Spirit. There is an equipping of character to bring us into like-mindedness with the Lord. We must know that to be baptized in the Holy Spirit is to leave our own lives, as it were, out of all questioning, to leave ourselves out of all pleasing, and in the name of Jesus to come into like-mindedness with Him.

How Jesus pleased God! How He brought heaven to earth, and all earth moved at the mightiness of the presence of heaven in the midst! We must see our calling in the Spirit, for God has chosen us. We must remember that it is a great choice.

Turning to the tenth chapter of Romans, we read,

> *And how shall they preach unless they are sent? As it is written: "How beautiful are the feet of those who preach the gospel of peace, who bring glad tidings of good things!"* (Romans 10:15)

We want to be sent. It is a great thing to be called by God to preach *"the unsearchable riches of Christ"* (Ephesians 3:8).

You have in this land, and we have in our land, men of note and of authority, who are looked to for answers to social problems. I often think that a statesman has a wonderful time, but not a time like a preacher. He only preaches about natural things, but the man who handles the Word of God preaches supernatural life and immortality that swallows up the natural life. When we come into this blessed life, we know that we are teaching principles and ideals that are for life eternal.

God has given to us in the Spirit. Behold, we are spiritual children today, and we must know that we have to be spiritual all the time. God forbid that we should ever be like the Galatian church in that after we have been in the Spirit, we come into the flesh. (See Galatians 3:3.) We are allowed to go into the Spirit, but we are never allowed to go into the flesh after we have been in the Spirit. And so, God gives such an idea of this high order in the Spirit so that we may be moved by its power to see how we may be strengthened and come into full faith in the Lord.

Let me turn to the first verse of this wonderful fourth chapter of Ephesians: *"I, therefore, the prisoner of the Lord, beseech you to walk worthy of the calling with which you were called."* When Paul wrote this, he was in prison. If I can take a word from anyone, I can take it from anyone who is in prison for taking a stand for the Word of God. I have never completely read a book except the Bible, but there are some things I have read in *The Pilgrim's Progress* that have helped me very much. It was when John Bunyan was in prison that God awakened him on so many wonderful lines of thought. How Paul must have read the Word right into the hearts of those who came and went when he was bound with chains for two full years. He could speak about a fullness, freedom, power, and joy although he was bound with chains.

Fellow believers, there is something in the Gospel that is different from anything else. These early believers could go through such hardships. Read the first epistle of Peter, and you will see how the early Christians were scattered. God says that the world wasn't worthy of the people He was filling with His power and that they were in dens and caves of the earth. (See Hebrews 11:38.)

Oh, brothers and sisters, there have been some wonderful gems that have passed through the world that have been touched by the Master's hand. There have been some wonderful men in the world who have caught the glory as the rays have shone from the Lord's lips by the power of His expression. As they beheld Him, they were fascinated with Him. And I can almost see, as Peter drew near the time of his departure, just what Jesus had said to him:

> *Most assuredly, I say to you, when you were younger, you girded yourself and walked where you wished; but when you are old, you will stretch out your hands, and another will gird you and carry you where you do not wish.* (John 21:18)

And as Peter drew near to the portals of glory, he wished to be crucified upside down. My word!

Our Calling: Part One

What grace incarnated in a human body that it should have such ideals of worship!

Oh, beloved, God is the essence of joy to us in a time when all seems barren, when it seems that nothing can help us but the light from heaven that is far brighter than the sun. Then that touches you, then that changes you, and you realize nothing is worthwhile but that.

LOWLINESS AND MEEKNESS

How Paul spoke to us from prison about *"the calling with which you were called, with all lowliness and gentleness"* (Ephesians 4:1–2). He spoke to the preacher. Let no person in this place think that he cannot become a preacher. Let none think he cannot reach this ideal of lowliness and meekness. God can bring us all to that place.

Some preachers get the idea that nobody ought to say a word until he is established. I, however, like to hear the bleating of the lambs. I like to hear the life of the young believers. I like to hear something coming right from heaven into the soul as they rise the first time with tears streaming from their eyes, telling of the love of Jesus.

The Holy Spirit fell upon a young man outside a church. He went into the church, where they were all very sedate. If anything were to move in that church out of the ordinary, my word, it would be extraordinary! And this young man, with his fullness of life and zeal for the Master, started shouting and praising the Lord and manifesting the joy of the Lord, and he disturbed the old saints.

In this church, an old man was reading the Psalms quietly one day. It touched the young Spirit-filled man who was sitting behind him. And the young man shouted, "Glory!" Said the old man, "Do you call that religion?"

The father of the young man was one of the deacons of the church. The other deacons gathered around him and said, "You must talk to your boy and make him understand that he has to wait until he is established before he manifests those things."

> There is no heart that can love like the heart that God has touched.

So the father had a long talk with the boy and told him what the deacons had said. "You know," he said, "I must respect the deacons, and they have told me they won't have this thing. You have to wait until you are established."

As they neared their home, their horse made a sudden and complete stop. The father tried to make it go forward or backward, but the horse would not move for anything.

"What is up with the horse?" asked the father of the boy. "Father," replied the boy, "this horse has gotten established."

Our Calling: Part One

I pray God the Holy Spirit that we will not get established in that way. God, loose us from these old, critical, long-faced, poisoned countenances, which haven't seen daylight for many days. Some come into the sanctuary and act in a terrible way. May the Lord save Pentecost from going to dry rot. Yes, deliver us from any line of sentimentality, anything that is not reality. For remember, we must have the reality of supernatural quickening until we are sane and active and not in any way dormant, but filled with life, God working in us mightily by His Spirit.

We must always be in a transforming position, not in a conforming condition, always renewing the mind, always being renovated by the mighty thoughts of God, always being brought into line with what God has said to us by the Spirit. *"This is the way, walk in it"* (Isaiah 30:21). *"Walk in the Spirit, and you shall not fulfill the lust of the flesh"* (Galatians 5:16).

Lord, how will we do it? Can a man be meek and lowly and filled with joy? Do these things work together? *"Out of the abundance of the heart the mouth speaks"* (Matthew 12:34). The depths of God come in with lowliness and meekness and cause the heart to love. There is no heart that can love like the heart that God has touched.

Oh, the love that is made to love the sinner! There is no love like it. I always feel I can spend any amount of time with the sinner. Oh, brother, there is a love that is God's love! There is a love that only comes by the principles of the Word of God. He loved us and gave Himself for us (Galatians 2:20).

When that meekness and lowliness of mind take hold, the preacher is moved by his Creator to speak from heart to heart and move the people. We must be moved by an inward power and an inward ideal of principles. We must have ideals that come from the throne of God. We must live in the throne, live on the throne, and let Him be enthroned, and then He will lift us to the throne.

An Interpretation of Tongues:
Out of the depths He has called us; into the heights He has brought us; unto the uttermost He has saved us, to make us kings and priests unto God. For we are His property, His own, His loved ones. Therefore, He wants to clothe us with the gifts of the Spirit and make us worthy for His ministry.

Glory to God! Thank the Lord!

A LOVE THAT BEARS WITH OTHERS

"With all lowliness and gentleness, with long-suffering, bearing with one another in love" (Ephesians 4:2).

Oh, how we need to bear *"with one another in love."* Oh, how this is contrary to hardness of heart, contrary to the evil powers, contrary to the natural mind. It is a divine revelation, and you cannot bear with others until you know how God has borne with you. It is God's love toward you that gives you tender, compassionate love toward one another.

It is only the broken, contrite heart that has received the mark of God. And it is only in that secluded place, where He speaks to you alone and encourages you when you are down and out. When no hand is stretched out to you, He stretches out His hand with mercy and brings you into a place of compassion. And then you cannot think evil; then you cannot in any way act harshly. God has brought you into longsuffering, with tenderness and with love.

> It is only the broken, contrite heart that has received the mark of God.

Oh, this love! Many times my two brothers have been under conviction and have wept under conviction as I have tried to bring them into the light. But up until now, neither of them is in the light. I believe that God will bring them.

In the church of God, where a soul is on fire, kindled with the love of God, there is a deeper love between me and that brother than there is between my earthly brother and me. Oh, this love that I am speaking about is divine love; it is not human love. It is higher than human love; it is more devoted to God. It will not betray. It is true in everything. You can depend on it. It won't change its character. In divine love, you will act exactly as He would act, for you will act with the same spirit. *"As He is, so are we in this world"* (1 John 4:17).

As you rise into association with Him in the Spirit, as you walk with Him *"in the light as He is in the light"* (1 John 1:7), then the fellowship becomes unique in all its plan. I pray that God will help us to understand it so that we will be able to be clothed upon as we have never been, with another majestic touch, with another ideal of heaven.

No one can love like God. And when He takes us into this divine love, we will precisely understand this word, this verse, for it is full of entreaty; it is full of passion and compassion; it has every touch of Jesus right in it. It is so lovely: *"With all lowliness and gentleness, with longsuffering, bearing with one another in love"* (Ephesians 4:2).

Isn't it glorious? You cannot find it anywhere else. You cannot get these pictures in any place you go. I challenge you to go into any library in the world and find words coined or brought forth like these words, unless they are copied from this Word. They aren't in nature's garden; they are in God's. It is the Spirit explaining, for He alone can explain this ideal of beatitudes. These words are marvelous; they are beautiful; they are full of grandeur; they are God's. Hallelujah!

I hope you are having a good time, for I am just being filled with new wine this morning. Oh, it is lovely!

KEEPING OUR EYES ON GOD

"Endeavoring to keep the unity of the Spirit in the bond of peace" (Ephesians 4:3). This is one of the main principles of this chapter in Ephesians. Beloved, let us keep in mind this very thought today. I am speaking this morning, by the grace of God, to the preacher. It should never be known that any preacher caused any distraction or detraction, or any split or disunion in a meeting. The preacher has lost his anointing and his glory if he ever stoops to anything that would weaken the assembly in any way.

The greatest weakness of any preacher is to draw men to himself. It is a fascinating point, but you must stay away from fascination. If you don't crucify your *"old man"* (Romans 6:6) in every area, you are not going into divine lines with God. When the people wanted to make Jesus king, He withdrew Himself to pray. Why? It was a human desire of the people. What did He want? His kingdom was a spiritual kingdom. He was to reign over demon powers. He was to have power over the passions of human life. He was to reign supremely over everything that is earthly, so that all the people might know that He was divine.

He is our pattern, beloved. When the people want to make anything of you, He will give you grace to refuse. The way to get out of it is to find that there is nothing in the earth that is worthy of Him, that there is no one in the world who is able to understand except Him, and that everything will crumble to the dust and become worthless. Only that which is divine will last.

Every time you draw anyone to yourself, this action has a touch of earth. It does not speak of the highest realm of the thoughts of God. There is something about it that cannot bear the light of the Word of God. Keep men's eyes off you, but get their eyes on the Lord. Live in the world without a touch or taint of any natural thing moving you. Live high in the order and authority of God, and see that everything is bearing you on to greater heights and depths and greater knowledge of the love of God.

When you are living this way, you will help any assembly you go to, and everybody will get a blessing and will see how much richer they are because you brought them Jesus. Only Jesus! He is too big for any assembly, and He is little enough to fill every heart. We will always go on to learn of Him. Whatever we know, the knowledge is so small compared with what He has to give us. And so, God's plan for us in giving us Jesus is all things, for all things consist in Him. *"All things were made through Him, and without Him nothing was made that was made"* (John 1:3). *"In Him we live and move and have our being"* (Acts 17:28). And when it is a spiritual being and an activity of holiness, see how wonderfully we grow in the Lord. Oh, it is just lovely!

An Interpretation of Tongues:
Yes, it is the Lord Himself. He comes forth, clothed upon, to clothe you in your weakness, to strengthen you in your helplessness, to uphold you in the limitation of your knowledge, to unfold the mysteries of the kingdom in the dire straits where two ways meet and you do not know where to go. He says, *'This is the way.'* When you are in such a distressing place that no hand but God is able to lead you out, then He comes to you and says, *"Be strong and fear not, for I am with you."*

Hallelujah! Praise the Lord of glory! He is the everlasting King and will reign forever and ever and ever. Glory! Glory! Amen!

An Interpretation of Tongues:
God has spoken, and He will make it clear, for He is in the midst of you to open your mind and reveal unto you all the mysteries of the kingdom, for the God of grace is with you. For God is greater than all unto you.

He is making your way straight before you, for the Lord is He who comforts you as He comforted Israel, and He will lead you into His power. His right hand is with you to keep you in all your ways lest you should dash your foot against a stone, for the Lord will uphold you.

How beautiful is the Scripture coming to us this morning! How lively it appears to us! And now we can understand something about the fourteenth chapter of 1 Corinthians:

> *I will pray with the spirit, and I will also pray with the understanding. I will sing with the spirit, and I will also sing with the understanding.* (1 Corinthians 14:15)

So God is bringing us right into the fullness of the Pentecostal power as it was given in the first days. God wants us to know that after we have been brought into this divine life with Christ, we are able to speak in the Spirit, and we are able to sing in the Spirit. We are also able to speak with the understanding and sing with the understanding. Ah, hallelujah! This is a good day!

KEEPING THE BODY IN PERFECT UNITY

I think I ought to say a few more words concerning Ephesians 4:3: *"Endeavoring to keep the unity of the Spirit in the bond of peace."* Beloved, I want you, above all things, to remember that the church is one body. She has many members, and we are all members of that one body. At any cost, we must not break up the body, but rather keep the body in perfect unity. Never try to get the applause of the people by any natural thing. Yours is a spiritual work. Yours has to be a spiritual breath. Your word has to be the Word of God. Your counsel to the church has to be such that it cannot be declared untrue. You have to have such solid, holy reverence in every area so that every time you handle anybody, you handle them for God, and you handle the church as the church of God. By that means, you keep the church bound together.

> At any cost, we must not break up the body, but rather keep the body in perfect unity.

As the people of the church are bound together in one Spirit, they grow into that temple in the Lord (see Ephesians 2:21), and they all have one voice, one desire, and one plan. And when they want souls saved, they are all of one mind. I am speaking now about spiritual power. If you get the people into the mind of the Spirit with Christ, all their desires will be the same as the desires of Christ the Head. And so nothing can break the church along those lines.

As a preacher, you must never try to save yourself along any line. You must always be above mentioning a financial matter on your side. Always mention your need before God in the secret place, but never bring it to an assembly. If you do, you drop in the estimation of the assembly. You are allowed to tell any need belonging to the assembly or the church management, but never refer to your personal need on the platform.

If a man preaches faith, he must live it, and a man is not supposed to preach unless he preaches a living faith. And he must so impress it upon the people that they will always know that God has taken him on for a special plan, and that he is not an ordinary man. After we are called by God and chosen for Him, we are not supposed to have ordinary men's plans. We ought to have God's ideals only.

Here is another thing that I think is perhaps more essential to you than anything else: you preachers, never drop into an assembly and say the Lord sent you, because sometimes the assembly has as much going on as she can manage. But it is right for you to get your orders from heaven. Never go unless you are really sent. Be sure that it is God who is sending you.

Brothers and sisters, can you be out of God's will when you hear His voice? *"My sheep hear My voice...and they follow Me"* (John 10:27). Oh, that God today will help us by the mind of the Spirit to understand. I believe God has a message on fire. He has men clothed by Him. He has men sent by Him. Will you be the men? Will you be the women?

You ask, "Can I be the man? Can I be the woman?" Yes. God says, *"Many are called, but few are chosen"* (Matthew 22:14). Are you the chosen ones? Those who desire to be chosen, will you allow God to choose you? Then He will put His hand upon you. And in the choice, He will give you wisdom; He will lead you forth; He will stand by you in the narrow place; He will lead you every step of the way, for the Lord's anointed will go forth and bring forth fruit, and their fruit will remain (John 15:16).

An Interpretation of Tongues:
Behold, now is the day of decision. Yield now while the moment of pressure by the presence of God comes. Yield now and make your consecration to God.

The altar is ready now for all who will obey.

seventeen

Our Calling:

Part Two

An Interpretation of Tongues:
The Lord is that Spirit that moves in the regenerated and brings us to the place where fire can begin and burn and separate and transform and make us all know that God has made an inroad into every order. We have to be divine, spiritual, changed, and on fire to catch all the rays of His life. First, burning out; second, transforming; and third, making us fit to live or die.

O h, thank God for that interpretation. To continue our subject of the last meeting, I want to turn your attention again to the fourth chapter of Ephesians. I will start with the first verse:

I, therefore, the prisoner of the Lord, beseech you to walk worthy of the calling with which you were called, with all lowliness and gentleness, with longsuffering, bearing with one another in love, endeavoring to keep the unity of the Spirit in the bond of peace. There is one body and one Spirit, just as you were called in one hope of your calling; one Lord, one faith, one baptism; one God and Father of all, who is above all, and through all, and in you all. But to each one of us grace was given according to the measure of Christ's gift. Therefore He says: "When He ascended on high, He led captivity captive, and gave gifts to men." (Now this, "He ascended"; what does it mean but that He also first descended into the lower parts of the earth? He who descended is also the One who ascended far above all the heavens, that He might fill all things.) And He Himself gave some to be apostles, some prophets, some evangelists, and some pastors and teachers, for the equipping of the saints for the work of ministry, for the edifying of the body of Christ, till we all come to the unity of the faith and of the knowledge of the Son of God, to a perfect man, to the measure of the stature of the fullness of Christ.

(Ephesians 4:1–13)

PASS IT ON

This morning, as on the previous morning, I believe that the Lord especially wants me to emphasize facts that will bless and strengthen preachers. If there is anything of importance, it is for preachers, because God must have preachers in the place of building and edifying the church. And preachers must be in that order of the Spirit in which God can work through them for the needs of the church.

As it was only out of the brokenness of Paul's life that blessing came forth, so it is out of the emptiness and brokenness and yieldedness of our lives that God can bring forth all His glories through us to others. And as one man said earlier in today's service, unless we pass on what we receive, we will lose it. If we didn't lose it, it would become stagnant.

> Virtue is always manifested through blessings that you have passed on.

Virtue is always manifested through blessings that you have passed on. Nothing will be of any importance to you except what you pass on to others. God wants us to be so in the order of the Spirit that when He breaks upon us the alabaster box of ointments, which represents the precious anointing that He has for every child of His, we will be filled with perfumes of holy incense for the sake of others. Then we may be poured out for others, others may receive the graces of the Spirit, and the entire church may be edified. And this church will never know one dry day, but there will always be freshness and life that make all of your hearts burn together as you know that the Lord has talked with you once more.

We must have this inward burning desire for more of God. We must not be at any stationary point. We must have the most powerful telescopes, looking at and hurrying toward what God has called us to, so that He may perfect that forever.

Oh, what a blessed inheritance of the Spirit God has for us in these days, so that we should no longer be barren or unfruitful, but rather filled with all fullness, increasing with all increasings, having a measureless measure of the might of the Spirit in the inner man, so that we are always like a great river that presses on and heals everything that it touches. Oh, let it be so today!

An Interpretation of Tongues:
The Lord has awakened in us the divine touches of His spiritual favor to make us know that He is here with all that you require if you are ready to take it.

But are we ready to take it? If we are, God can give us wonderful things. We must be always hungry, always ready for every touch of God.

WHAT IT MEANS TO BE A PEACEMAKER

In the first part of this sermon, if you remember, we were dwelling upon Ephesians 4:3:

"Endeavoring to keep the unity of the Spirit in the bond of peace." It was a very precious word to us because it meant that under any circumstances we would not have our own way but God's way. We have God's way for the person and for the church.

Of all the things God intends for us to be, He intends for us to be peacemakers. Yes, He wants us to have a pure love, a love that always helps someone else at its own expense. I won't find a Scripture to help me in this area as much as this one:

> *Therefore if you bring your gift to the altar, and there remember that your brother has something against you, leave your gift there before the altar, and go your way. First be reconciled to your brother, and then come and offer your gift.* (Matthew 5:23–24)

Most Christians are satisfied with the first meaning of this passage, but the second meaning is deeper. Most people believe it is perfectly right, if you have offended another, to go to that person and say, "Please forgive me," and you win your brother when you take that part. But this is the deeper sense: *"If you...remember that your brother has something against you,"* go and forgive him his transgressions. It is so much deeper than getting your own side right to go and get his side right by forgiving him of all that he has done.

That will be a stepping stone to very rich grace in the area of keeping *"the unity of the Spirit in the bond of peace"* (Ephesians 4:3). Someone may say, "I cannot forgive them because she did that and he said that. You know, he didn't recognize me at all. And he hasn't smiled at me for at least six months." Poor thing! May God help you through evil reports and good reports. (See 2 Corinthians 6:4, 8). God can take us right through if we get to the right side of grace.

My brother, when you get to the place of forgiving your brother who has something against you, you will find that that is the greatest ideal of going on to perfection, and the Lord will help us *"to keep the unity of the Spirit in the bond of peace"* (Ephesians 4:3).

I like that *"bond of peace."* It is an inward bond between you and another child of God. *"Bond of peace."* Hallelujah! Oh, glory to God!

ONE BODY

"There is one body and one Spirit, just as you were called in one hope of your calling" (Ephesians 4:4). We must recognize that there is only one body. It seems to me that at one time God would have made such an inroad of truth into all nations through the Plymouth Brethren, if they had only recognized that there were more people in the body than just the Plymouth Brethren. You will never gain interest unless you see that in every church there is a nucleus that has as real a God as you have.

It is only along these lines, I believe, that the longsuffering of God waits for the precious fruit. (See James 5:7.) The longsuffering of God is with the believers who have the idea that only those in their church are right, or those in their city, or those in their country. It is all foolishness.

It is foolishness for fancy people to sit around their table and think that their table is the only table. What about the hundreds of people I know who are sitting around their tables every day and are partaking of the bread and the wine? Brother, the body of Christ consists of all who are in Christ.

While we know the Holy Spirit is the only power that can take the church up, we also know that the Holy Spirit will go with the church. The Scriptures are very definite in saying that all who are Christ's at His coming will be changed. It seems that we cannot be all Christ's unless something is done, and God will sweep away so many things that are spoiling things. We must reach the place of perfect love, and we will see that God can make even those in Caesar's household a part of His family. (See Philippians 4:22.) Glory to God!

An Interpretation of Tongues:

It is the Spirit that joins us and makes us one. It is the health of the Spirit that goes through the body, that quickens the body and makes it appear as one.

Our Calling: Part Two

Oh, the body appearing as one body! Oh, the entire body possessing the same joy, the same peace, the same hope! No division, all one in Christ! What a body! Who can make a body like that? It seems to me that this body is made deep in the Cross. Hundreds of people are carrying a cross around their necks. I could never carry a cross. Christ has carried the cross; He has borne the shame. I find that right there in that atoning blood is cleansing and purifying. The blood takes away all impurities and everything that will mar the vessel. God is making a vessel for honor, fit for the Master's use (see 2 Timothy 2:21), joined with that body—one body.

> God is making a vessel for honor, fit for the Master's use, joined with that body— one body.

Let us be careful that we do not in any way defile the body, because God is chastening the body and fitting it together and bringing it together. The body of Christ will rise. You ask, "How will it rise?" It will rise in millions and billions and trillions, more than any man can number. It will be a perfect body.

Oh, there is one body! It is a lovely body. I look at you; I see you. I look in your faces, and I know there is a closer association than one can tell or speak about. Oh, beloved, there is something deeper down in the spirit of the regenerated person when the impurities of life and of the flesh fall off. Oh, there is a resemblance, a likeness, a perfection of holiness, of love! O God, take away the weaknesses and all the depravities.

"Now you are the body of Christ, and members individually ['*in particular,*' KJV]" (1 Corinthians 12:27). I like the word *"particular"*; it tells us that there is just the right place for us. God sees us in that place. He is making us fit in that place so that for all time we will have a wonderful place in that body. Ah, it is so lovely!

Oh, these exhaustless things! Brothers, sisters, it isn't the message; it is the heart. It isn't the heart; it is the Christ. It isn't the Christ; it is the God. It isn't the God; it is the whole body. This is deeper than we have any conception of!

THE CALLING

"There is one body and one Spirit, just as you were called in one hope of your calling" (Ephesians 4:4). I feel that God would have me say a word about the calling. Many people who are called miss the call because they are dull of hearing. There is something in the call, beloved. *"Many are called, but few are chosen"* (Matthew 22:14). I want a big heart this morning to believe that all will be chosen. You ask, "Can it be so?" Yes, beloved, it can—not a few chosen, but many chosen.

And how will the choice be made? The choice is always your choice first. You will find that gifts are your choice first. You will find that salvation is your choice. God has made it all, but you have to choose. And so God wants you especially this morning to make an inward call, to be in a great intercessory condition of imploring the Holy One to prepare you for that wonderful spiritual body.

Called! Beloved, I know that some people have the idea (and it is a great mistake) that because they are not successful in everything they touch, because they have failed in so many things that they desire to go forward in, because they don't seem to aspire in prayer as some do and perhaps don't enter into the fullness of tongues, there is no hope for them in this calling. Satan comes and says, "Look at that black list of your weaknesses and infirmities! You can never expect to be in that calling!"

Yes, you can, beloved! God says it in the Scriptures. Oh, beloved, it is the weakness that is made strong! It is the last who can be made first. (See Matthew 19:30.) What will make the whole situation different? Confessing our helplessness. God says that He feeds the hungry with good things, but the satisfied He sends away empty. (See Luke 1:53.) If you want to grow in grace and in the knowledge of the grace of God, get hungry enough to be fed; get thirsty enough to cry out; be broken enough that you do not want anything in the world unless He comes Himself.

I was reading last night in my Bible—it was so lovely—that *"God will wipe away every tear from their eyes"* (Revelation 21:4). Ah, you say, that will be in heaven. Thank God that it will also be here. Hallelujah! Let God do it this morning. Let Him wipe away all tears. Let Him comfort your heart. Let Him strengthen your weakness. Let Him cause you to come into the place of profit. Let Him help you into the place He has chosen for you, for *"many are called, but few are chosen"* (Matthew 22:14). But God has a big choice.

Our Jesus is a big Jesus! If I could measure Him, He would be very small. But I cannot measure Him, and I know He is very large. I am glad I cannot measure Jesus, but I am glad I can touch Him all the same.

ONE BAPTISM

Ephesians 4:5 says, *"One Lord, one faith, one baptism."* I must touch on the thought of baptism this morning. We must get away from the thought of water baptism when we are in the Epistles. If water baptism is at all mentioned in any way in the Epistles, it is always mentioned in the past tense.

Always remember this, beloved: While water baptism, in my opinion, is essential—*"He who believes and is baptized will be saved"* (Mark 16:16)— I wouldn't say for a moment that a man could not be saved unless he was baptized in water, because that statement would be contrary to Scripture.

I see there is a blending. In John's gospel, we find that *"unless one is born of water and the Spirit, he cannot enter the kingdom of God"* (John 3:5). I believe God would have us know that we never ought to put aside water baptism. On the contrary, we ought to believe it is in perfect conjunction and in operation with the working of the Spirit so that we may be buried with Christ. (See Romans 6:4.)

But, the baptism in the Holy Spirit! The baptism of fire! The baptism of power! The baptism of oneness! The baptism of association! The baptism of communion! This is the baptism of the Spirit of life that takes the man, shakes him up, builds him up, and makes him know he is a new creature in the Spirit, worshiping God in the Spirit.

> The baptism of the Spirit of life takes the man, shakes him up, builds him up, and makes him a new creature.

If my preaching and the preaching of those who come on this platform emphasize the baptism with the Holy Spirit, and you have only touches of it, if you stop at that, it will be almost as though you are missing the calling.

John said by the Spirit, *"He who comes after me is preferred before me"* (John 1:15). He also said, *"I indeed baptize you with water unto repentance, but He who is coming after me is mightier than I....He will baptize you with the Holy Spirit and fire"* (Matthew 3:11).

By all means, if you can tarry, you ought to tarry. (See Luke 24:49.) If you have the Spirit's power upon you, go into that room or somewhere else and never cease until God finishes the work. Churches outside the Pentecostal church that don't have a revival spirit, that don't have people being born again, become dead, dry, barren, and helpless. They enter into entertainment and all kinds of social functions. They live on a natural association and lose their grand, glorious hope.

Now I want to talk about the Pentecostal church. Unless the Pentecostal church is having an increase along the lines of salvation, unless it is continually having baptisms in the Holy Spirit, the Pentecostal church will become dry, lukewarm, and helpless, and you will wonder what church it is.

But, if every night somebody stands up to testify that he has received the Holy Spirit, and if others say, "Oh, last night I was saved," that church is ripening. She will not flounder. She is ripening for greater things, for God will take that church.

Beloved, you are responsible for this; the platform is not responsible. The whole church is responsible to keep this place on fire. If you are baptized with the Holy Spirit and you have come into this meeting without an anointing upon you, without being so ready that you feel like bursting into tongues, without having a psalm, hymn, or some spiritual song—unless you have a tongue or interpretation, or unless something is taking place along these lines—you have fallen from the grace of the Pentecostal position.

You talk about a message. God has given us a message this morning if you dare to hear it. We dare to say in the open air and everywhere that we are Pentecostal. If we are Pentecostal, we will be biblical Pentecostals. What is the definition of "biblical Pentecostals"? It is found in 1 Corinthians 14:26:

How is it then, brethren? Whenever you come together, each of you has a psalm, has a teaching, has a tongue, has a revelation, has an interpretation. Let all things be done for edification.

This verse was instruction for a Pentecostal continuance in the Corinthian church. Suppose that what was happening in the Corinthian church was the case of our own Pentecostal church. It would not be possible for sinners to come in without being saved, or for people not having the baptism to come in without becoming hungry and thirsty to come into that fullness. It must be so. God must bring us to a place where we do not have merely a name, but where we have the position that brings the name.

How many of you felt like speaking in tongues as you came into the room this morning? Praise God, there are some. How many of you have a psalm burning in you and feel like singing it in the streets? Praise God, that is very good. How many of you sang a hymn as you came in? Praise the Lord, glory to God! You are doing very well. But don't you see that this is what we have to continue? There has to be a continuance of such things.

An Interpretation of Tongues:
The hope of the church is springing up by the Spirit through the Word. Therefore, as many of you as are living in the Spirit are putting to death the flesh. You are quickened by the Spirit and live in the realms of His grace.

Praise the Lord, it is the grace of our Lord Jesus. Hallelujah! We can sing, "I will never be cross anymore." Beloved, it is the most wonderful thing on earth when God touches you with this new life in the Spirit. Then, whether you are in a car, a ship, or train, it doesn't matter where you are because you are in the Spirit; you are ready to be caught up.

Oh, beloved, here we are this morning, *"one body"* (Ephesians 4:4). Praise the Lord! There is *"one Spirit"* (verse 4). There is *"one baptism"* (verse 5). I am crying to God for these meetings because I believe God can do a great thing in a moment when we are all brought into the line of the Spirit. I wouldn't be surprised no matter what happened.

I was in ten days of meetings in which the attention was on the gifts, and the people got so worked up, as it were, in the Spirit that they felt something new had to happen or else they couldn't live. And it happened. I believe these and other meetings are bringing us to a place of great expectancy.

ONE FAITH

"One Lord, one faith, one baptism" (Ephesians 4:5). Just in the proportion that you have the Spirit unfolding to you "one Lord, one faith, one baptism," you have the Holy Spirit incarnated in you, bringing into you a revelation of the Word. Nothing else can reveal the Word, for the Spirit gave the Word through Jesus. Jesus spoke by the Spirit that was in Him, He being the Word. The Spirit brought out all the Word of this life. We must have the Spirit. If you look in John's gospel, you will find that when the Spirit came, He didn't come to speak about Himself but to bring forth all Jesus said. (See John 16:13–14.)

Just as we have the measure of the Spirit, there will be no measure of unbelief. We will have faith. The church will rise to the highest position when there is no schism in the body along the lines of unbelief. When we all, with one heart and one faith, believe the Word as it is spoken, then signs and wonders and various miracles will be manifested everywhere. This is one accord: *"One Lord, one faith, one baptism"* (Ephesians 4:5). Hallelujah!

ABOVE ALL, THROUGH ALL, AND IN YOU ALL

I think that the next verse is probably one of the primary verses of all: *"One God and Father of all, who is above all, and through all, and in you all"* (verse 6). If this spiritual life is in us, we will find that we have no fear. We will have no nervous condition; it will vanish. Every time you have fear, it is imperfect love. Every time you have nervous weaknesses, you will find it is a departure from an inner circle of true faith in God. We read in 1 John 4:18, *"There is no fear in love; but perfect love casts out fear, because fear involves torment. But he who fears has not been made perfect in love."*

There is also a very good word in the sixteenth verse of the same chapter: *"God is love, and he who abides in love abides in God, and God in him."* Where is the man who abides in God? He is swallowed up in God. And when God takes hold of us along these lines, it is remarkable to see that we are encircled and overshadowed by Him.

An Interpretation of Tongues:
I feel we must magnify the Lord in the Spirit.

Our Calling: Part Two

"One God and Father of all, who is above all, and through all, and in you all" (Ephesians 4:6). God is over all. Take a long look at that. Think about God being through all. See if any satanic powers can work against you. But just think about another fact: He is in you all. How can the Devil have a chance with the body when God is in you all? Hallelujah! Glory!

Don't you see the groundwork, the great base, the rock of the principles of these Scriptures, how they make us know that we are not barren, that we cannot be unfruitful, but that we must always be abounding in

> If this spiritual life is in us, we will find that we have no fear; it vanishes in the presence of perfect love.

the joy of the Lord? We lack because we are short of truth.

When this truth of God lays hold of a man, he is no longer a man. What is he? He is a divine construction. He has a new perception of the ideals of God. He has a new measurement. Now he sees that God is over all things. Now he sees that God is through all things. The whole world can join in a league of nations—they can do as they like—but the Word of God abides forever.

"In you all" (Ephesians 4:6). Think of that. God is in you all. Who is God? Who is the Holy Spirit? Who is Jesus? Is it possible to have any

conception of the mightiness of the power of God? And yet you take the thoughts of Jesus and see that all the embodiment of the fullness was right in Him. And I have Him. I have the Holy Spirit also, who is as great in equality, for those three are one and are joined equally in power. They are perfectly one.

When the Spirit comes in the body, how many are in the body? You have Jesus, the Holy Spirit, and God. Hallelujah! Talk about Samson carrying the gates! (See Judges 16:3.) If you know your position, you will take both the gates and the city. Go in and possess every part of the land, for surely there is a land of gladness, a land of pleasure, a land of peace.

And remember, brothers and sisters, when the Holy Spirit gets an end of us, and we just operate by the Spirit's power and utter the Spirit's words, we find out it is always more and more and more. Oh yes, we will magnify the Lord on all these lines. If we don't, the stones will begin to cry out against us. (See Luke 19:40.)

THE MEASURE OF CHRIST'S GIFT

"But to each one of us grace was given according to the measure of Christ's gift" (Ephesians 4:7). This is a great summing up. Oh, beloved, I wish you to see Jesus this morning, because if we don't see Him, we miss a great deal. Grace and gifts are equally abounding in Him. It is as you

set your strength on Jesus, it is as you allow the Holy Spirit to penetrate every thought, always bringing on the canvas of the mind a perfect picture of holiness, purity, and righteousness, that you enter into Him and become entitled to all the riches of God.

How do you measure up this morning? God gives a measure. Oh, this is a lovely word: *"But to each one of us grace was given according to the measure of Christ's gift."*

I know that salvation, while it is a perfect work, is an insulation that may have any number of volts behind it. In the days when bare wires were laid, when electric power was obtained from Niagara, I am told that there was a city whose lights suddenly went out. Following the wires, the repairmen came to a place where a cat had gotten on the wires, and the lights had been stopped.

I find that the dynamo of heaven can be stopped with a smaller thing than a cat. An impure thought stops the circulation. An act can stop the growth of the believer. I like this verse:

> *For the word of God is living and powerful, and sharper than any two-edged sword, piercing even to the division of soul and spirit, and of joints and marrow, and is a discerner of the thoughts and intents of the heart.* (Hebrews 4:12)

Then I find these words in 2 Corinthians to be so precious:

Casting down arguments and every high thing that exalts itself against the knowledge of God, bringing every thought into captivity to the obedience of Christ.
(2 Corinthians 10:5)

So I find that if I am going to have all the revelations of Jesus brought to me, I am going to attain to all that God has for me through a pure and clean heart, right thoughts, and an inward affection toward Him. Then heaven bursts through my human frame, and all the rays of heaven flow through my body. Hallelujah! It is lovely!

The measure of the gift of Christ remains with you. I cannot go on with inspiration unless I am going on with God in perfection. I cannot know the mind of the natural and the mysteries of the hidden things with God unless I have power to penetrate everything between heaven and me. And there is nothing that goes through but a pure heart, for the pure in heart will see God. (See Matthew 5:8.)

Oh, it is lovely! And I see that the pure heart can come into such closeness with God that the graces are so enriched and the measure of Christ so increased that one knows that he is going on to possess all things.

Our Calling: Part Two

Nothing comes to my mind that is as beautiful as a soul just developing in his first love and wanting to preach to all people. In Revelation, one church is reproved for having lost its first love. (See Revelation 2:1–7.) And I believe that God would have us to know that this first love, the great love that Jesus gives us with which to love others, is the primary stepping stone to all these things that we have looked at this morning. I don't know whether there is anyone here who has never lost that first love.

I love the preacher. I love the young man. Oh, how I love the youth who is developing in his character and longing to become a preacher. If you ask me whether I have a preference, I will say, "Yes, I have a preference for a young preacher." I love them. God has perfect positions of development for the preacher.

> God has never been able to make goodness except out of helplessness, lest we should glory in the flesh.

The young preacher may have greater inward longings to get people saved than he has power over his depravities. And he is hindered in his pursuit into this grandeur of God. I want to take you to a place where there is wonderful safety and security.

God will take into captivity the young life—or the old life—that is longing to preach the glories of Christ but is captive to weaknesses, to failures, and to the power of Satan that has interfered with him. God will take him into captivity if he will let Him, for God has gifts for him. He takes the captive into captivity and surrounds him, keeps him, chastens him, purifies him, cleanses him, washes him. And He is making prophets, apostles, and evangelists of such.

God has never been able to make goodness except out of helplessness, lest we should glory in the flesh. God destroys every bit of flesh so that no flesh can glory in His sight. (See 1 Corinthians 1:29.) If we have any glory, we will glory in the Lord. (See verse 31.)

Do you want to be preachers? Truly, I know you do. There isn't a child in this place who does not want to bear glad tidings. *"How beautiful are the feet of those who preach the gospel of peace, who bring glad tidings of good things!"* (Romans 10:15). Oh, glad tidings! What does it mean? Eternal salvation. You talk about gold mines and diamonds and precious stones! Oh, my brother, to save one soul from death! Oh, to be the means of saving many! God has for us a richer treasure than we have any idea of. Don't say you cannot reach it, brother or sister. Never look at yourself; get a great vision of the Master. Let His love so penetrate you that you will absolutely make everything death but Him. And as you see Him in His glory, you will see how God can take you.

Our Calling: Part Two

I believe that there are many in this place whom God is taking hold of this morning. My brother, don't fail God, but by the measure of faith in Christ, let your hand be outstretched; let your eye be fixed with an eternal fixedness; let an inward passion grip you with the same zeal that gripped the Lord. Let your mind forget all the past. Come into like-mindedness with Jesus, and let Him clothe you.

GOD PERFECTS HIS PEOPLE

"Therefore He says: 'When He ascended on high, He led captivity captive, and gave gifts to men'" (Ephesians 4:8). He has gifts for men. You ask, "What kind of men?" Even for rebels. Did they desire to be rebels? No. Sometimes there are transgressions that break our hearts and make us groan and travail. Was it our desire to sin? No. God looks right at the very canvas of your whole life history, and He has set His mind upon you.

I would like you preachers to know that *"eye has not seen, nor ear heard, nor have entered into the heart of man the things which God has prepared for those who love Him"* (1 Corinthians 2:9). Your weakness has to be sifted like the chaff before the wind, and every corn will bring forth pure grain after God's mind. The fire will burn like an oven to burn up the stubble (see Malachi 4:1), but the wheat will be gathered into the granary, the treasury of the Most High God, and He Himself will lay hold of us.

What is this process for? For the perfecting of the saints. Oh, just think—that brokenness of yours is to be made whole like Him; that weakness of yours is to be made strong like Him! You have to bear the image of the Lord in every detail. You have to have the mind of Christ (see Philippians 2:5) in perfection, in beauty.

Beloved, don't fail and shrivel because of the hand of God upon you, but think that God must purify you for the perfecting of the saints. Oh, Jesus will help us. Oh, beloved, what are you going to do with this golden opportunity, with this inward pressure of a cry of God in your soul? Are you going to let others be crowned while you lose the crown? Are you willing to be brought into captivity today for God?

Truly, this morning must decide some things. If you are not baptized, you must seek the baptism of the Spirit of God. And if there is anything that has marred the fruit or interfered with all of His plan, I implore you this morning to let the blood so cover, let the anointing of Christ so come, let the vision of Christ be so seen, that you will have a measure that will take all that God has for you.

eighteen

You Are Our Epistle:

Part One

od's Word is very beautiful and very expressive. I want to read to you this morning the entire third chapter of 2 Corinthians:

Do we begin again to commend ourselves? Or do we need, as some others, epistles of commendation to you or letters of commendation from you? You are our epistle written in our hearts, known and read by all men; clearly you are an epistle of Christ, ministered by us, written not with ink but by the Spirit of the living God, not on tablets of stone but on tablets of flesh, that is, of the heart. And we have such trust through Christ toward God. Not that we are sufficient of ourselves to think of anything as being from ourselves, but our sufficiency is from God, who also made us sufficient as ministers of the new covenant, not of the letter but of the Spirit; for the letter kills, but the Spirit gives life. But if the ministry of death, written and engraved on stones,

was glorious, so that the children of Israel could not look steadily at the face of Moses because of the glory of his countenance, which glory was passing away, how will the ministry of the Spirit not be more glorious? For if the ministry of condemnation had glory, the ministry of righteousness exceeds much more in glory. For even what was made glorious had no glory in this respect, because of the glory that excels. For if what is passing away was glorious, what remains is much more glorious. Therefore, since we have such hope, we use great boldness of speech; unlike Moses, who put a veil over his face so that the children of Israel could not look steadily at the end of what was passing away. But their minds were blinded. For until this day the same veil remains unlifted in the reading of the Old Testament, because the veil is taken away in Christ. But even to this day, when Moses is read, a veil lies on their heart. Nevertheless when one turns to the Lord, the veil is taken away. Now the Lord is the Spirit; and where the Spirit of the Lord is, there is liberty. But we all, with unveiled face, beholding as in a mirror the glory of the Lord, are being transformed into the same image from glory to glory, just as by the Spirit of the Lord.

(2 Corinthians 3:1–18)

You Are Our Epistle: Part One

We have this morning one of those high-water marks of very deep things of God in the Spirit. I believe the Lord will reveal these truths to us, as our hearts are open and responsive to the Spirit's leadings.

Do not think that you will receive anything from the Lord except along the lines of a spiritual revelation, for there is nothing that will profit you, or bring you to a place of blessing, except that which denounces or brings to death the natural order so that the supernatural plan of God may be in perfect order in you.

> If we are going to catch the very best of God, there must be an open ear, an understanding heart. The veil must be lifted.

The Lord of Hosts encamps all around us with songs of deliverance (see Psalm 34:7) so that we may see face to face the glories of His grace in a new way. For God has not brought us into *"cunningly devised fables"* (2 Peter 1:16), but in these days He is rolling away the mists and clouds and every difficulty so that we may understand the mind and will of God.

If we are going to catch the very best of God, there must be in this meeting a spiritual desire, an open ear, an understanding heart. The veil must be lifted. We must see the Lord in that perfection of being glorified in the midst of us. As we enter into these things of the Spirit, we must clearly see that we are not going to be able to understand these mysteries that God is unfolding to us unless we are filled with the Holy Spirit.

Even when these special meetings close, the pastor and everybody else will find that we must grow in grace all the time. We must see that God has nothing for us along the old lines. The new plan, the new revelation, the new victories are before us. The ground must be gained; supernatural things must be attained. All carnal things, evil powers, and spiritual wickedness in high places (see Ephesians 6:12) must be dethroned. We must come into the line of the Spirit by the will of God in these days.

THE WORD OF GOD IN US

Let us turn to the Word, which is very beautiful and expressive in so many ways.

> *Do we begin again to commend ourselves? Or do we need, as some others, epistles of commendation to you or letters of commendation from you? You are our epistle written in our hearts, known and read by all men; clearly you are an epistle of Christ, ministered by us, written not with ink but by the Spirit of the living God, not on tablets of stone but on tablets of flesh, that is, of the heart. And we have such trust through Christ toward God.*
>
> (2 Corinthians 3:1–4)

You Are Our Epistle: Part One

This morning I want to dwell upon these words for a short time: *"Clearly you are an epistle of Christ."*

What an ideal position that now the sons of God are being manifested; now the glory is being seen; now the Word of God is becoming an expressed purpose in life until the life has ceased and the Word has begun to live in God's children.

This position was truly in the life of Paul when he came to a climax and said,

> *I have been crucified with Christ; it is no longer I who live, but Christ lives in me; and the life which I now live in the flesh I live by faith in the Son of God, who loved me and gave Himself for me.*
>
> (Galatians 2:20)

How can Christ live in you? There is no way for Christ to live in you except by the manifested Word in you, through you, manifestly declaring every day that you are a living epistle of the Word of God. Beloved, God would have us see that no man is perfected or equipped in any area except as the living Word abides in him.

It is the living Christ; it is the divine likeness to God; it is the express image of Him. The Word is the only factor that works out and brings forth in you these glories of identification between you and Christ. It is the Word richly dwelling in your hearts by faith. (See Colossians 3:16.)

We may begin at Genesis and go right through the Scriptures and be able to rehearse them, but unless they are a living power within us, they will be a dead letter. Everything that comes to us must be quickened by the Spirit. *"The letter kills, but the Spirit gives life"* (2 Corinthians 3:6).

We must have life in everything. Who knows how to pray except as the Spirit prays? (See Romans 8:26.) What kind of prayer does the Spirit pray? The Spirit always brings to your remembrance the Scriptures, and He brings forth all your cries and your needs better than your words. The Spirit always takes the Word of God and brings your heart, mind, soul, cry, and need into the presence of God.

So we are not able to pray except as the Spirit prays, and the Spirit only prays according to the will of God (see Romans 8:27), and the will of God is all in the Word of God. No man is able to speak according to the mind of God and bring forth the deep things of God by his own mind. The following Scripture rightly divides the Word of Truth:

> *Clearly you are an epistle of Christ, ministered by us, written not with ink but by the Spirit of the living God, not on tablets of stone but on tablets of flesh, that is, of the heart.* (2 Corinthians 3:3)

God, help us to understand this, for it is out of the heart that all things proceed. (See Matthew 12:34.) When we have entered in with God into the mind of the Spirit, we will find that God enraptures our hearts.

"Or do you think that the Scripture says in vain, 'The Spirit who dwells in us yearns jealously'?" (James 4:5). I have been pondering over that for years, but now I can see that the Holy Spirit very graciously, very extravagantly, puts everything to one side so that He may enrapture our hearts with a great inward cry for Jesus. The Holy Spirit *"yearns jealously"* for us to have all the divine will of God in Christ Jesus right in our hearts.

> When God gets into the depths of our hearts, He purifies every intention of our thoughts and even our joys.

When I speak about the *"tablets of flesh, that is, of the heart"* (2 Corinthians 3:3), I mean the inward love. Nothing is as sweet to me as to know that the heart yearns with compassion. Eyes may see, ears may hear, but you may be immovable on those two lines unless you have an inward cry where *"deep calls unto deep"* (Psalm 42:7). When God gets into the depths of our hearts, He purifies every intention of our thoughts and even our joys. We are told in the Word that it is *"joy inexpressible and full of glory"* (1 Peter 1:8).

Beloved, it is true that the commandments were written on tablets of stone. Moses, like a great big loving father over Israel, had a heart full of joy because God had shown him a plan by which Israel could partake of great things through these commandments. But God says that now the epistle of Christ is *"not on tablets of stone"* (2 Corinthians 3:3), which made the face of Moses shine with great joy. It is deeper than that, more wonderful than that: the commandments are in our hearts; the deep love of God is in our hearts; the deep movings of eternity are rolling in and bringing God in. Hallelujah!

Oh, beloved, let God the Holy Spirit have His way today in unfolding to us all the grandeurs of His glory.

An Interpretation of Tongues:
The Spirit, He Himself, it is He who wakes you morning by morning and unfolds to you in your heart, tenderness, compassion, and love toward your Maker until you weep before Him and say to Him in the Spirit, "You are mine! You are mine!"

Yes, He is mine! Beloved, He is mine!

OUR TRUST MUST BE IN GOD

And we have such trust through Christ toward God. Not that we are sufficient of ourselves to think of anything as being from ourselves, but our sufficiency is from God. (2 Corinthians 3:4–5)

Ah, those verses are lovely! We should keep them in mind and read them again later. Beloved, that is a climax of divine exaltation that is very different from human exaltation.

> The end is not yet, praise the Lord!
>> The end is not yet, praise the Lord!
> Your blessings He is bestowing,
>> And my cup is overflowing,
> And the end is not yet, praise the Lord!

We need to get to a place where we are beyond trusting in ourselves. Beloved, there is so much failure in self-assurances. It is not bad to have good things along the lines of satisfaction, but we must never rest upon anything in the human. There is only one sure place to rest upon, and our trust is in God.

In His name we go. In Him we trust. And God brings us the victory. When we have no confidence in ourselves, when we do not trust in ourselves, but when our whole trust rests upon the authority of the mighty God, He has promised to be with us at all times, and to make the path straight, and to make a way through all the mountains. Then we understand how it was that David could say, *"Your gentleness has made me great"* (2 Samuel 22:36).

Ah, God is the lover of souls! We have no confidence in the flesh. Our confidence can only be placed in and rest upon the One who never fails, the One who knows the end from the beginning, the One who is able to come in at the midnight hour as easily as at midday. In fact, God makes the night and the day alike to the man who rests completely in His will with the knowledge that *"all things work together for good to those who love God"* (Romans 8:28) and trust in Him. And we have such trust in Him.

This is the worthy position; this is where God wants all souls to be. We would find that we would not run His errands and make mistakes; we would not be settling down in the wrong place. We would find that our lives were as surely in agreement with the thoughts of God as the leading of the children of Israel through the wilderness. And we would be able to say, *"Not one good thing has the Lord withheld from me"* (Psalm 84:11), and, *"All the promises of God in Him are Yes, and in Him Amen, to the glory of God through us"* (2 Corinthians 1:20).

The Lord has helped me to have no confidence in myself, but to wholly trust in Him. Bless His name!

LIVING IN THE SPIRIT

[God] *also made us sufficient as ministers of the new covenant, not of the letter but of the Spirit; for the letter kills, but the Spirit gives life. But if the ministry of death, written and engraved on stones, was glorious, so that the children of Israel could not look steadily at the face of Moses because of the glory of his countenance, which glory was passing away, how will the ministry of the Spirit not be more glorious? For if the ministry of condemnation had glory, the ministry of righteousness exceeds much more in glory.* (2 Corinthians 3:6–9)

Let us reverently think on these great words. If I go on with God, He wants me to understand all His deep things. He doesn't want anybody in the Pentecostal church to be a novice or to deal with the Word of God on natural grounds. We can understand the Word of God only by the Spirit of God.

We cannot define, separate, or deeply investigate and unfold this holy plan of God unless we have the life of God, the thought of God, the Spirit of God, and the revelation of God. The Word of Truth is pure, spiritual, and divine. If you try to discern it on natural grounds, you will only finish up on natural lines for natural man, but you will never satisfy a Pentecostal assembly.

The people who are spiritual can only be fed with spiritual material. So if you are expecting your message to catch fire during the meeting, you will have to bring it on fire to the meeting. You won't have to light up the message during the meeting; you will have to bring the message red-hot, burning, living. The message must be directly from heaven. It must be as truly *"Thus says the Lord"* as the Scriptures that are *"Thus says the Lord,"* because then you will speak only as the Spirit gives utterance, and you will always be giving fresh revelation. You will never be stale; whatever you say will be fruitful, elevating the mind, lifting the people, and all the people will want more.

To come into this, we must see that we not only need the baptism of the Spirit, but we also need to come to a place where there is only the baptism of the Spirit left. Look at the first verse of the fourth chapter of Luke, and you will catch this beautiful truth: *"Then Jesus, being filled with the Holy Spirit, returned from the Jordan and was led by the Spirit into the wilderness."* But look at Mark 1:12, and you will find that He was driven by the Spirit into the wilderness: *"Immediately the Spirit drove Him into the wilderness."*

> We can understand the Word of God only by the Spirit of God.

In John's gospel, Jesus says He does not speak or act of Himself: *"The words that I speak to you I do not speak on My own authority; but the Father who dwells in Me does the works"* (John 14:10).

You Are Our Epistle: Part One

We must know that the baptism of the Spirit immerses us into an intensity of zeal, into a likeness to Jesus; it makes us into pure, liquid metal so hot for God that it travels like oil from vessel to vessel. This divine line of the Spirit will let us see that we have ceased and we have begun. We are at the end for a beginning.

There isn't a thing in the world that can help us in this meeting. There isn't a natural thought that can be of any use here. There isn't a thing that is carnal, earthly, or natural that can ever live in these meetings. There is only one pronouncement for carnal things: they have to die eternally. There is no other plan for a baptized soul.

God, help us to see that we may be filled with the letter without being filled with the Spirit. We may be filled with knowledge without having divine knowledge. And we may be filled with wonderful natural things and still remain natural men. But we cannot remain natural men in this truth that I am dealing with this morning. No man is able to walk this way unless he is in the Spirit. He must live in the Spirit, and he must realize all the time that he is growing in that same ideal of his Master, in season and out of season, always beholding the face of the Master, Jesus.

David said, *"I foresaw the Lord always before my face, for He is at my right hand, that I may not be shaken. Therefore...my tongue was glad"* (Acts 2:25–26). Praise the Lord!

OLD THINGS HAVE PASSED AWAY

For even what was made glorious had no glory in this respect, because of the glory that excels. For if what is passing away was glorious, what remains is much more glorious. (2 Corinthians 3:10–11)

I notice here that the one has to pass away, and the other has to increase.

One day I was having a good time speaking about this third chapter of 2 Corinthians. I was speaking to a lot of people who were living on the Thirty-nine Articles (doctrinal statements of the Church of England) and infant baptism and all kinds of things. The Lord showed me that all these things had to pass away. I find there is no way into the further plan of God unless you absolutely put them to one side. *"Passing away."*

Is it possible to do away with the commandments? Yes and no. If they have not so passed away with you that you have no consciousness of keeping commandments, then they have not passed away. If you know that you are living in holiness, you don't know what holiness is. If you know that you are keeping commandments, you don't know what keeping commandments is.

These things have passed away. God has brought us in to be holy without knowing it, and to keep the whole truth without knowing it—living in it, moving in it, acting in it—a new creation in the Spirit. The old things have passed away. If there is any trouble in you at all, it shows that you have not come to the place where you are at rest.

"Passing away." God, help us to see it. If the teaching is a bit too high for you, ask the Lord to open your eyes so that you can come into it. For there is no man here who has power in prayer, or has power in life with God, if he is trying to keep the commandments. They have passed away, brother. And thank God, the very doing away with them is fixing them deeper in our hearts than ever before. For out of the depths we cry unto God (see Psalm 130:1), and in the depths He has turned righteousness in and uncleanness out. It is out of the depths that we cry unto God in these things. May God lead all of us every step of the way in His divine leading.

nineteen

You Are Our Epistle:

Part Two

This is a continuation of my previous sermon by the same title. I am going to commence with the sixth verse of the third chapter of 2 Corinthians:

[God] *also made us sufficient as ministers of the new covenant, not of the letter but of the Spirit; for the letter kills, but the Spirit gives life. But if the ministry of death, written and engraved on stones, was glorious, so that the children of Israel could not look steadily at the face of Moses because of the glory of his countenance, which glory was passing away, how will the ministry of the Spirit not be more glorious? For if the ministry of condemnation had glory, the ministry of righteousness exceeds much more in glory. For even what was made glorious had no glory in this respect, because of*

the glory that excels. For if what is passing away was glorious, what remains is much more glorious. Therefore, since we have such hope, we use great boldness of speech; unlike Moses, who put a veil over his face so that the children of Israel could not look steadily at the end of what was passing away. But their minds were blinded. For until this day the same veil remains unlifted in the reading of the Old Testament, because the veil is taken away in Christ. But even to this day, when Moses is read, a veil lies on their heart. Nevertheless when one turns to the Lord, the veil is taken away. Now the Lord is the Spirit; and where the Spirit of the Lord is, there is liberty. But we all, with unveiled face, beholding as in a mirror the glory of the Lord, are being transformed into the same image from glory to glory, just as by the Spirit of the Lord.
(2 Corinthians 3:6–18)

Think about that: even the glory that was on the face of Moses had to pass away. For what? For something that had greater glory. I am positive we have no conception of the depths and heights of the liberties and blessings and incarnations of the Spirit. We must attain to these positions of godliness, and we must be partakers of His divine nature. (See 2 Peter 1:4.) Praise the Lord!

WE DELIGHT TO DO GOD'S WILL

How will the ministry of the Spirit not be more glorious? For if the ministry of condemnation had glory, the ministry of righteousness exceeds much more in glory.

(2 Corinthians 3:8–9)

May the Lord help us now in this. I see the truth as it was brought to the Israelites in the law. Paul had something to glory in when he kept the law and was blameless, but he said he threw that to one side to win Him who is even greater than that. (See Philippians 3:8.)

Now we come to the truth of this: what is in the law that isn't glorious? Nothing. It was so glorious that Moses was filled with joy in the expectation of what it was. But what is ours in the excellence of glory? It is this: we live, we move, we reign over all things. It isn't "Do, do, do"; it is "Will, will, will." I rejoice to do. It is no longer *"Thou shalt not"*; it is *"I will." "I delight to do Your will, O my God"* (Psalm 40:8)! So the glory is far exceeding. And, beloved, in our hearts there is exceeding glory. Oh, the joy of this celestial touch this morning!

An Interpretation of Tongues:
The living God, who is chastening us after this manner, is always building us after His manner so that there may be no spot in us. For the Lord Himself has designed the

plan, is working out in us His divine mind, and is taking the man and transforming him in this plan until he loses his identity in the mighty God of possibilities.

Hallelujah! We praise You, O God. And we will praise You forever.

Far above all,
Far above all,
God hath exalted Him,
Far above all.

Amen! Glory to God! Thank God for that interpretation. I will be glad to read that, for I don't know what I said. I only know the joy of it.

Oh yes, the glory is exceeding. The glory is excellent. When Peter was describing that wonderful day on the Mount of Transfiguration, he said, *"Such a voice came to Him* [Christ] *from the Excellent Glory"* (2 Peter 1:17). And so we are hearing this morning from the Excellent Glory. It is so lovely.

If I were to come to you this morning and say, "Whatever you do, you must try to be holy," I would miss it. I would be altogether outside of this plan. But this morning by the Holy Spirit, I take the words of the epistle that says, *"Be holy"* (1 Peter 1:16).

It is as easy as possible to be holy, but you can never be holy by trying to be. But when you lose your heart and Another takes your heart, and you lose your desires and He takes the desires, then you live in that sunshine of bliss that no mortal can ever touch.

Divine immortality swallows up all natural mortality. And God wants us to see that we have to be entirely eaten up by His holy zeal so that every day we walk in the Spirit. It is lovely to walk in the Spirit; then we will not fulfill any part of the law without the Spirit causing us to dwell in safety, rejoice inwardly, praise God reverently, and know that we are an increasing force of immortality swallowing up life. Hallelujah!

Ah, it is lovely! As the song says, "I will never be cross anymore." Beloved, it is impossible to go on with God and have the old life reappearing. Glory to God!

BEAUTIFUL RIGHTEOUSNESS

"For if the ministry of condemnation had glory, the ministry of righteousness exceeds much more in glory" (2 Corinthians 3:9). This is a beautiful verse. I want to speak about "righteousness" now. There is nothing as beautiful as righteousness. You cannot touch these beatitudes we are dwelling upon this morning without seeing that the excellent glory exists right in Christ. All the excellent glory is in Him. All righteousness is in Him.

Everything that pertains to holiness and godliness, everything that denounces and brings to death the natural, everything that makes you know you have ceased to be forever, is always in the knowledge of an endless power in the risen Christ. And we have come into an endless power of the risen Christ.

I want you to notice that there is an excellent glory about Christ's power. Whenever you look at Jesus, you can look at so many different facts of His life. I see Him in those forty days with wonderful truth, which was an infallible proof of His ministry. What was the ministry of Christ? When you come to the very essence of His ministry, it was the righteousness of His purpose. The excellence of His ministry was the glory that covered Him. His Word was convincing, inflexible, divine, with a personality of an eternal endurance. It never failed.

> Nothing is as beautiful as righteousness. You need to see that this excellent glory exists only in Christ.

Oh, the righteousness of God. If Christ said it, it was there. He said it, and it stood fast. (See Psalm 33:9.) It was an unchangeable condition with Him. When God spoke, it was done. (See verse 9.) And His righteousness abides. God must have us in this place of righteousness. We must be people of our word. People ought to be able to depend on our word.

If there were only five saved in a meeting, we should never say there were six. If there were five baptized, we should never say there were seven. If the building holds five hundred people, we should never say it was packed and had a thousand in it. God is establishing righteousness in our hearts so that we will not exaggerate about anything.

Jesus was true inwardly and outwardly. He is *"the way, the truth, and the life"* (John 14:6), and on these things we can build; on these things we can pray; on these things we can live. When we know that our own hearts do not condemn us, we can say to the mountain, *"Be removed"* (Matthew 21:21). (See 1 John 3:21–22.) But when our own hearts condemn us, there is no power in prayer, no power in preaching, no power in anything. We are just sounding brass and clanging cymbals. (See 1 Corinthians 13:1.)

May God the Holy Spirit show us there must be a ministry of righteousness. We ought to stand by our word and abide by it. If we were cut in two, our persecutors should find pure gold right through us. That is what I call righteousness. Jesus was righteousness through and through. He is lovely! Oh, truly, He is beautiful!

One thing God wants to fix in our hearts is to be like Him. Be like Him in character. Don't be troubled so much about your faces, but be more concerned about your hearts. Makeup won't change the heart. All the adorning of silks and satins won't create purity. Beloved, if I was going down a road and I saw a foxtail sticking out of a hole, I wouldn't ask anybody what was inside. And if there is anything hanging outside of us, we know what is inside. God wants righteousness in the inward parts, purity through and through.

Listen! There is an excellent glory attached to the ministry of righteousness. We read, *"For if the ministry of condemnation had glory, the ministry of righteousness exceeds much more in glory"* (2 Corinthians 3:9).

The Bible is the plumb line of everything. And unless we are lined right up with the Word of God, we will fail in the measure in which we are not righteous. And so, may God the Holy Spirit bring us this morning into that blessed ministry of righteousness. Amen! Glory to God!

A HEAVENLY CITIZENSHIP

"For even what was made glorious had no glory in this respect, because of the glory that excels" (2 Corinthians 3:10). Ah, brother, this verse is truly of God! You couldn't say anything else. You have to get right behind this blessed Word and say it is of God. Just for a moment let us glance at this, for it is a beautiful word: *"For even what was made glorious had no glory in this respect, because of the glory that excels."*

Come again right to the law. I see that it was truly a schoolmaster that brought us to Christ. (See Galatians 3:24.) I like the thought that law is beautiful, that law is established in the earth. As far as possible, in every country and town, you will find that the law has something to do with keeping things in order. And to a certain degree, the city has some kind of sobriety because of the law.

But, beloved, we belong to a higher, nobler citizenship, and it isn't an earthly citizenship, for *"our citizenship is in heaven"* (Philippians 3:20). So we must see that there is an excellent glory about this position we are holding this morning. For if the natural law will keep an earthly city in somewhat moderate conditions, what will the excellent glory be in the divine relationship of the citizenship to which we belong?

I call it an excellent glory because it outshines. It makes all the people feel a longing to go. What there is about the excellent glory is this: the earth is filled with broken hearts, but the excellent glory is filled with redeemed men and women, filled with the excellency of the graces of the glory of God. Oh, the excellent glory is marvelous! Ah, praise the Lord, O my soul! Hallelujah!

PLAIN PREACHING

For if what is passing away was glorious, what remains is much more glorious. Therefore, since we have such hope, we use great boldness ["plainness," KJV] of speech; unlike Moses, who put a veil over his face so that the children of Israel could not look steadily at the end of what was passing away. (2 Corinthians 3:11–13)

Yesterday morning I was preaching to preachers, but we can see that this message is for the perfecting of preachers. The man who is going on with God will have no mix-up in his oratory. He will be so plain and precise and so divine in his leadings that everything will lift toward the glory. And his hearers will always realize that he will not play around to satisfy human curiosity. He must have his mind upon higher things altogether, and he must see that God would not have him loiter about. He must *"use great plainness of speech"* (verse 12 KJV). He must be a man who knows his message. He must know what God has in His mind in the Spirit, not in the letter, because no man who is going to speak by the Spirit of God knows what God is going to say in the meeting.

The preacher is a vessel for honor, God's mouthpiece. And therefore, he stands in the presence of God, and God speaks and uses him. But listen! God is a Spirit who works within the human life with thought, might, truth, and life. The Spirit transfers power from the great treasury of His mightiness to the human life, to the heart, and sends His might right through onto the canvas of the mind, and the language comes out according to the operation of the Spirit of God.

Beloved, should we any longer try any lines but the divine? Every man is not in the same order, but I could say to the man with faith that, as a spiritual orator, there is a touch of faith for that man to come into. He has to forget all he has written in his notes because of a higher order of notes.

> The preacher is a vessel for honor, God's mouthpiece.

I always say that you cannot sing the song of victory in a minor key. And you never can have a spiritual horizon on a low note. If your life isn't at a constant pitch, you will never ring the bells of heaven. You must always be in tune with God, and then the music will come out as sweetly as possible.

Let's get away from going into libraries and filling our minds with human theology. We have the Bible, which is better than any book in any library.

I am not here for any other purpose than for the glory of God. God forbid! I have known so many people who have been barren and helpless, and they have used other people's material on the platform. If you ever turn to another man's material, you have dropped from the higher sense of an orator from heaven.

You Are Our Epistle: Part Two

We must now be the mouthpieces of God, not by letter, but by Spirit. And we must be so in the will of God that God rejoices over us with singing. (See Zephaniah 3:17.) Isn't it lovely? We are going forward a little.

A GREAT DAY FOR THE JEWS

Let us look again at the third chapter of 2 Corinthians:

> Moses...put a veil over his face so that the children of Israel could not look steadily at the end of what was passing away. But their minds were blinded. For until this day the same veil remains unlifted in the reading of the Old Testament, because the veil is taken away in Christ.
>
> (2 Corinthians 3:13–14)

I have nothing to say about Jews except this: I know I am saved by the blood of a Jew. I owe my Bible to the Jews, for the Jews have kept it for us. We have a Savior who was a Jew. The first proclamation of the Gospel was by the Jews. I know that I owe everything to the Jews today, but I see that they will never have the key to unlock the Scriptures until they see Jesus. The moment they do, they will see this truth that Jesus gave to Peter:

> And I also say to you that you are Peter, and on this rock I will build my church....

*And I will give you the keys of the king-
dom of heaven* (Matthew 16:18–19)

Jesus was saying, "I will give you the key of
truth, the key to unveil." The key was brought in
the moment Peter saw the Lord. (See verse 16.)
The moment the Jews see Christ, the whole of
the Scriptures will be opened to them. It will be a
great day when the Jews see the Lord. They will
see Him!

TOUCHING THE HEART

*But their minds were blinded. For until
this day the same veil remains unlifted in
the reading of the Old Testament, because
the veil is taken away in Christ. But even
to this day, when Moses is read, a veil lies
on their heart.* (2 Corinthians 3:14–15)

God doesn't say that the veil is upon their
mind, but upon their heart. And, beloved, God
can never save a man through his mind. He saves
him through his heart. God can never bring all
the glories into a man's life by his mind. He must
touch the deep things of his heart.

THE PROPER USE OF LIBERTY

*Nevertheless when one turns to the Lord,
the veil is taken away. Now the Lord is the
Spirit; and where the Spirit of the Lord is,
there is liberty. But we all, with unveiled*

face, beholding as in a mirror the glory of the Lord, are being transformed into the same image from glory to glory, just as by the Spirit of the Lord.

(2 Corinthians 3:16–18)

I must speak about liberty first. We must never use liberty, but we must be in the place where liberty can use us. If we use liberty, we will be as dead as possible, and our efforts will all end with a fizzle. But if we are in the Spirit, the Lord of Life is the same Spirit. I believe it is right to jump for joy, but don't jump until the joy makes you jump, because if you do, you will jump flat. If you jump as the joy makes you jump, you will bounce up again.

In the Spirit, I know there is any amount of divine plan. If Pentecostal people had only come into this plan in meekness and in the true knowledge of God, it would all be so manifest that every heart in the meeting would be moved by the Spirit.

"Now the Lord is the Spirit; and where the Spirit of the Lord is, there is liberty" (verse 17). Liberty has a thousand sides to it, but there is no liberty that is going to help the people as much as testimony. I find people who don't know how to testify properly. We must testify only as the Spirit gives utterance. We find in the book of Revelation that *"the testimony of Jesus is the spirit of prophecy"* (Revelation 19:10).

Sometimes our flesh keeps us down, but our hearts are so full that they lift us up. Have you ever been like that? The flesh is fastening you to your seat, but your heart is bubbling over. At last the heart has more power, and you stand up. And then in that heart affection for Jesus, in the Spirit of love and in the knowledge of truth, you begin to testify, and when you are done, you sit down. Liberty used wrongly goes on after you have finished saying what God wants you to say, and it spoils the meeting. You are not to use your liberty except for the glory of God.

> Sometimes our flesh weighs us down, but our hearts are so full that they lift us up.

So many churches are spoiled by long prayers and long testimonies. The speaker can tell, if he stays in the Spirit, when he should sit down. When you begin to speak your own words, the people get tired and wish that you would sit down. The anointing ceases, and you sit down worse than when you rose up.

It is nice for a man to begin cold and warm up as he goes on. When he catches fire and sits down in the midst of it, he will keep the fire afterward. Look! It is lovely to pray, and it is a joy to hear you pray, but when you go on and on after you are truly done, all the people get tired of it.

You Are Our Epistle: Part Two

So God wants us to know that we are not to use liberty because we have it to use, but we are to let the liberty use us, and we should know when to end.

This excellent glory should go on to a liberality to everybody, and this would prove that all the church is in liberty. The church ought to be free so that the people always go away feeling, "Oh, I wish the meeting had gone on for another hour," or, "What a glorious time we had at that prayer meeting!" or, "Wasn't that testimony meeting a revelation!" That is the way to finish up. Never finish up with something too long; finish up with something too short. Then everybody comes again to pick up where they left off.

FROM GLORY TO GLORY

The last verse of our text is the most glorious of all for us:

But we all, with unveiled face, beholding as in a mirror the glory of the Lord, are being transformed into the same image from glory to glory, just as by the Spirit of the Lord. (2 Corinthians 3:18)

So there are glories upon glories, and joys upon joys, exceeding joys and an abundance of joys, and a measureless measure. Beloved, when we get the Word so wonderfully into our hearts, it absolutely changes us in everything. And we so feast on the Word of the Lord, so eat and digest the truth, so inwardly eat of Him, until we are absolutely changed every day from one state to another.

As we look into the perfect mirror of the face of the Lord, we are changed from one state of grace to another, *"from glory to glory."* You will never find anything else except the Word of God to take you there. So you cannot afford to put aside the Word.

I implore you, beloved, that you do not come short in your own lives of any of these blessed teachings we have been speaking of. These grand truths of the Word of God must be your testimony, must be your life, must be your pattern. You must be in the Word; in fact, you are of the Word. God says to you by the Spirit that *"you are an epistle of Christ"* (2 Corinthians 3:3). Let us see to it that we put off everything so that by the grace of God we may put on everything.

Where there is a standard that hasn't been reached in your life, God, in His grace, by His mercy and your yieldedness, can equip you for that place. He can prepare you for that place that you can never be prepared for except by a broken heart and a contrite spirit, except by yielding to the will of God. If you will come with a whole heart to the throne of grace, God will meet you and build you on His spiritual plane. Amen. Praise the Lord!